KA

D0505171

# ROB SMYTH

# KAISER!

## THE GREATEST FOOTBALLER NEVER
## TO PLAY FOOTBALL

YELLOW JERSEY PRESS
LONDON

Yellow                                           ›up

First published by Yellow Jersey Press in 2018

www.vintage-books.co.uk

A CIP catalogue record for this book is available from the British Library

ISBN 9781787290259

Typeset in 12/17 pt Fairfield LH
by Integra Software Services Pvt. Ltd, Pondicherry

Printed and bound in Great Britain by Clays Ltd, Elcograf S.p.A.

Penguin Random House is committed to a sustainable future for
our business, our readers and our planet. This book is made
from Forest Stewardship Council® certified paper.

MIX
Paper from
responsible sources
FSC® C018179

To Carlos Alberto Torres, a sheer delightful human being.

# CONTENTS

*'I hope that my truth pleases you, because there are many truths, many truths. It's up to you to decide which is the true truth'* – Ronaldo Luís Nazário de Lima, talking to Congress about his convulsion on the day of the 1998 World Cup final

# CHAPTER 1

# THE STAR SIGNING

Carlos Kaiser wasn't in the mood to play football. The journey from Rio de Janeiro to Corsica had taken the best part of twenty-four hours, during which the only thing in danger of going to sleep were his squashed legs. This was just a fleeting visit, a chance to survey his new kingdom before he introduced himself to his hotel bed. He hadn't expected a welcome like this. The Stade Mezzavia, home of Gazélec Ajaccio FC, was heaving with anticipation. Hundreds of fans had congregated on the austere concrete terrace behind one of the goals, keen to see the unveiling of the club's new Brazilian forward.

Word had spread around Corsica about Kaiser's CV. He'd played for Botafogo, Flamengo and Fluminense, three of the biggest clubs in Brazil, and been world champion with Independiente of Argentina. Kaiser stifled a yawn and waved to the supporters. 'I bet,' he thought to himself, 'they didn't get this excited when Napoleon came home.'

At twenty-four, Kaiser was approaching his peak. He'd been recommended to Ajaccio by his friend Fabinho, who had joined the club a year earlier. And though Kaiser had been struggling with a succession of niggling injuries for a couple of years, an explosive video of his goals suggested he was well worth the gamble – especially for a mid-table Ligue 2 side. In their seventy-seven-year history, Ajaccio had never signed a player of this stature.

Kaiser decided that, as everyone had made such an effort to greet him, he should put on a bit of a show.

'Fabinho, get me a bunch of flowers,' he said.

'Kaiser, this is a football stadium in the middle of nowhere. Where am I going to get flowers?'

'I've been here five minutes and you're asking me where to get flowers? Use your initiative.'

Fabinho tutted and set off on his errand. When he returned ten minutes later with a handful of roses, procured from the secretary's office, Kaiser took them and ran towards the touchline. He jumped over the advertising boards, clambered up the cheap seats and ostentatiously presented the flowers to the wife of the club president.

Kaiser dispensed hugs and kisses to anyone in sight before returning to the field, where he grabbed a Corsican flag and used it as a cape. He had been told that Corsicans, like Basques in Spain, were fiercely independent.

Kaiser's internal monologue celebrated a triumphant unveiling. The serious business – the actual football – was still to come. He noted that a surprising proportion of the crowd were female, and his mind started to wander. Kaiser had an image of Corsica in his head. He saw a bohemian, enlightened milieu, populated by brunettes in pastel-coloured, roll-neck jumpers, smoking pencil-thin cigarettes and teaching him about the Impressionists before seducing him behind sheer linen curtains that billowed in the breeze. He was starting to lose himself when, in his peripheral vision, he noticed a squat old man dragging out a bag of footballs. Kaiser, using Fabinho as a translator, asked what was happening. The answer distressed him. The owners wanted Kaiser to show off his exotic skills to the crowd.

Kaiser was interested in keeping up appearances, not doing keepy-uppies. He started moaning to nobody in particular, still speaking in Portuguese. 'I flew in on a fucking sardine can and have hardly got any feeling in my legs. Can't we do this tomorrow?' As Kaiser harrumphed, a series of balls were lined up on the edge of the penalty area.

'Fabinho,' he said, 'could you go and get my sunglasses? They're in the Mizuno bag in the dressing room. Thanks, man.'

When Fabinho departed, Kaiser jogged towards the line of footballs and hoofed one into the crowd. 'A souvenir,' he explained in Portuguese, calculating that nobody else spoke the language. While everyone tried to work out what Kaiser was saying, he hammered ball after ball into the crowd.

'I got a standing ovation,' says Kaiser thirty years later. 'It was intentional, so that I didn't have to train. The kit guy kept one ball because he said there was going to be a training session. I grabbed that off him and belted it into the crowd as well. The fans all left with their souvenirs and there were no balls left.'

With none of the supporters wanting to give back their expensive souvenir, the management team decided to call it a day. Kaiser raised both hands above his head and clenched his fists triumphantly before walking towards the dressing room, his work done. He hadn't been in the mood to play football. What he knew, and what nobody at Ajaccio could ever know, was that their star signing was never in the mood to play football.

# CHAPTER 2

# THE ALTER EGO

Carlos Kaiser was born at the age of ten. Until then he was a chubby, football-mad kid called Carlos Henrique Raposo, who came into the world kicking and scheming on 2 July 1963. 'Carlos Henrique is a man,' he says. 'Carlos Kaiser is a character. I created that alter ego when I went to play for Botafogo. I promised myself I was going to be somebody. I wanted to show that a kid who came from a tough upbringing could be respected by society.'

A tough upbringing, and a bizarre one. Kaiser was born in Porto Alegre, in the south of Brazil, and was barely a week old when he was adopted – though that's a generous term for what actually happened. His biological mother asked a stranger to look after her baby for five minutes while she dealt with an emergency. She never returned. The stranger, desperate for a child of her own, was in Porto Alegre visiting family. They suggested it was a sign from above and that, rather than go to the police, she should keep the child. A few days later she made the 1600km journey home to Rio de Janeiro with her newfound baby.

As he grew up Kaiser wondered why he was white, like his father, when his mum was black. His parents eventually explained his backstory. He later heard from some of his extended family that his biological father was a famous politician who had an affair with a maid, and that he was discarded so that their relationship remained a secret. Another version is that Kaiser was stolen from his biological mother in Porto Alegre. With Kaiser, there are usually a few sides to every story.

Kaiser didn't care too much about the past. He had enough on his plate sorting out the future. His childhood was a gradual realisation of the desperate need to escape poverty by any means possible. In 1970s Brazil that was especially tricky – according to different studies, somewhere between 40 and 70 per cent of the population were classified as living in poverty. There wasn't a gap between rich and poor; it was more of a chasm.

The unique landscape of Rio offered a visual demonstration of that inequality. The backdrop to luxury beachside residences was provided by a giant, sloping maze of poverty. Favelas, the overpopulated shanty towns later introduced to the world in the film *City of God*, expanded enormously in the 1970s in response to a rural exodus across the country.

Although Kaiser did not live in a favela, his lifestyle was essentially that of a favelado. He grew up on Mena Barreto Street in an area called *Cabeça de Porco* ('Pig's Head') that was located between two favelas.

'It was a really poor neighbourhood,' says Kaiser. 'Rundown houses, surrounded by favelas. Violence everywhere. There were a lot of black people in my family who wouldn't back away from a fight. I learned Muay Thai [Thai boxing], so I could hold my own. You become used to living with that kind of violence, with that struggle for survival. I was always involved with the mischievous kids in a good and bad sense.'

The young Kaiser had simple hobbies. He played marbles, flew kites, dodged traffic to win bets and, for his Sunday afternoon treat, sneaked into the cinema without paying. Most of all, he played football. The matches were umpteen-a-side, played on any space the kids could find: long, grass-less patches of earth, steep hills, unpaved streets. The fact the matches were such chaotic free-for-alls forced players to develop fast feet and even faster brains to find and exploit any space. It's no wonder Brazilian players made football look so easy when they had the luxury of playing eleven-a-side games on grass. 'Brazil is an inexhaustible factory of amazing talent,' said Carlos Alberto Torres, the captain of the 1970 World Cup winners. 'It used to be the case even more. We would be churning out players every day.'

Only a few of the local boys owned a football, so much of the time there was a need to improvise. Anything vaguely spherical could be used as a ball, from rolled-up socks to mouldy fruit. Most of the kids played barefoot and topless, as if to advertise the naked talent on display. The most difficult opponents were often the rocks and potholes that caused nasty injuries, and blisters and glass splinters were an inevitable hazard. Kaiser played every day until his feet stung with pleasure.

\*\*\*

It was compulsory for a Brazilian child to be obsessed with football. They were the undisputed kings of the game, having won three out of four World Cups between 1958 and 1970. Those victories redefined the country – helping it shed what the playwright, journalist and novelist Nelson Rodrigues called the 'mongrel-dog complex' – and also the sport. Brazilian football is the cover version that surpassed the original, a pulsing samba remix of a game invented in Britain.

Football became a vital part of Brazil's national identity, even more so when a military dictatorship ruled the country from 1964 to 1985. In that time, the 1970 team won the World Cup in Mexico with a style of football that looks contemporary almost fifty years later. They played the game with industrial quantities of *ginga*: an indefinable and almost mystical quality of movement and attitude possessed by Brazilians. It's in the way they walk, talk, dance and, yes, play football.

'Brazilian football is like an art form,' says Bebeto, the waspish forward who starred in Brazil's World Cup win in 1994. 'It's technically brilliant. The creativity and skill of Brazilian players is indisputable. Everybody plays with joy and love.' A bit of lust, too. At its best the Brazilian game is a euphoric fusion of sport, dance, art and sex. And everyone's at it.

The lack of expensive equipment made it the most democratic of games, and one of the few areas of Brazilian life in which everyone was equal. Football in Brazil may have started as an upper-class sport but it was soon claimed by the masses. It became a kind of natural lottery – if you were born with talent, you could escape the favela or wherever you grew up. That dream sustained millions of children around the country, and Kaiser was no exception.

His escape began during a kickabout one Sunday in December 1973. 'There were two men watching the game,' he remembers, 'and they asked my dad who the kid with big hair was. He said, "That's my son." They were scouts from Botafogo and told him to bring me to the training ground at 7 a.m. the following day for a trial. I didn't even have boots. They gave me boots that were too big.'

He would never again be too small for his boots. The trial with Botafogo helped spawn an alter ego with an excess of arrogance and swagger. The name of this new character was inspired by Franz Beckenbauer, the elegant West German sweeper who seemed to play international football with a resting heart rate. His imperious demeanour was such that he was known as *Der Kaiser*. He had been a star of the 1966 and 1970 World Cups and, though they were not televised in Brazil, young football fans had seen Beckenbauer in the greatest theatre of all: the imagination.

'The kids in the kickabout compared me to Beckenbauer,' says Kaiser. 'Being ignorant, they couldn't pronounce his name but they found out his nickname was Kaiser. They, not me, thought the way I played resembled him. Kaiser, the king of German football. The Pelé of German football. I didn't give myself the Kaiser mantle. But I'm proud. Who wouldn't be when compared to Beckenbauer? I never heard of anybody else in football called Kaiser.'

The nickname gave Kaiser instant respect. A black and white-striped shirt gave him even more. It was the official property of Botafogo FR, who had provided the core of the Brazil teams that won those World Cups in 1958 and 1962. Five Botafogo players started the 3-1 win over

Czechoslovakia in the 1962 final: Garrincha, Didi, Nilton Santos, Amarildo and Mario Zagallo.

Botafogo are the smallest of Rio's big four – Flamengo, Fluminense and Vasco da Gama are the others – but their part in Brazil's emergence as a football nation gave them a prestige that will never fade. And they were the club of Garrincha, the tragic genius of world football. If Garrincha was a right-winger, then the club are also associated with left-wingers. They are the most romantic club in Rio, beloved of many artists and intellectuals.

Kaiser, like his father, was already a fan of the club, not least because his uncle had played for Botafogo alongside Garrincha and Nilton Santos. His hero was Jairzinho, the muscular forward who scored in every round of the 1970 World Cup.

Kaiser impressed during his trial at Botafogo and was asked to stay at the club on an informal basis. Within a week he had gone from the street to the holy ground: the iconic Maracanã Stadium. Kaiser played in the prestigious Father Christmas game, a junior's match that was part of a citywide festive celebration that included floats, fireworks and a circus. Botafogo beat Flamengo, with Kaiser scoring the winning goal from the penalty spot. The game was watched by over 200,000 people.

A couple of weeks later, Kaiser could not believe his luck when he saw Jairzinho at the Botafogo training ground. He spent a couple of minutes chatting to him and boasted about it at school, as any excitable fanboy would. The response was not what he expected.

'Kaiser, man, shouting at him from a hundred yards away doesn't count as a conversation!'

Kaiser discreetly ground his teeth into his bottom lip. On the way home from school he stole a camera from a local shop and put it in his Botafogo kitbag. When he next saw Jairzinho, Kaiser asked if he could get a picture of them together. When the camera film was eventually developed, Kaiser put the picture in the pocket of his school trousers and strutted into school as he had never strutted before.

'Lads, I had another chat with Jairzinho last week. He even said I was a natural goalscorer.'

'Kaiser! Give it up, man. Was Pelé there as well? Have you been out flying kites with Tostão? Or playing marbles with Clodoaldo?'

Kaiser produced the photo of him with his arm round one of Brazil's greatest footballers. The reaction of his classmates was somewhere between shock and awe. Over the next few weeks, Kaiser noticed how his association with Jairzinho had improved his status with both the boys and the girls at school. He had been popular enough before but now everyone wanted to talk to him about life at Botafogo. Of all the lessons he learned at school, this would be the most important.

# CHAPTER 3

# THE *MALANDRO*

Kaiser's story could only have happened in one place. He is an extreme personification of the roguish charm of one of the most vibrant, vivid places on earth. Rio de Janeiro is a unique microclimate of mischief, passion and optimism; a sensory overload of noise and colour that is powered by the highest voltage of social electricity.

That's the bit that's in the brochure, anyway. Rio is a city of two faces. There are severe levels of poverty, violence, misogyny and corruption, much of it in the favelas. But while they may not be out of sight, they are generally out of mind for those who consider themselves the social elite.

Yet even in the grimmest favela there is a buoyancy and zest for life that is typical of Cariocas, the name given to residents of Rio. Cariocas are tactical and unfettered; they talk with their hands, eyes and hips as well as their mouths. Emotionally and physically they live in a permanent state of semi-nakedness. Rio is not a place for the shy or the body-conscious. When a teenage Kaiser started to discover the beaches of Rio, he was like a kid in a sweet shop – one stocked with wall-to-wall eye candy.

The inequality of Rio, and the overwhelming allure of its good side, makes it a kind of holiday destination even for those who live there. The mundane or miserable parts of life disappear at the touch of a toe on sand. At its best, Rio is the kind of place that makes you think you've died and gone to utopia. The endless beaches, full of blissful white sand, are surrounded by awesome granite mountains and tropical forests. Overlooking everything is Cristo Redentor – Christ the Redeemer, the 125-foot statue of Jesus with his arms outstretched that stands on top of Corcovado Mountain.

Cristo is in the eye of the beholder. To some it's a simple symbol of Catholicism or Christianity; to others, his open arms reflect Rio's welcoming nature. It is the high point in a city that has more iconic landmarks than some continents. The list includes Sugarloaf Mountain, the Botanical Gardens – and the Maracanã, the home of football. And there is beach weather all year round. No wonder it is known as *Cidade Maravilhosa*, the Marvellous City.

The environment has shaped a culture that is informal, laid back and unhurried. Promptness is as much a vice as a virtue; a rigid work ethic is almost an affront to an environment that could have been custom-designed for hedonism.

Joel Santana knows about life in Rio. As a coach he has won the Campeonato Carioca, the state championship, with the four biggest clubs: Botafogo, Flamengo, Fluminense and Vasco da Gama. 'Rio de Janeiro is a special state,' he says 'Cariocas are more free, relaxed, fun. Everybody gets on with their lives. The environment is conducive to it: a lot of beach, a lot of samba, a lot of drums. A good Carioca is somebody who knows how to live life. It's different from other states. That's why other people end up criticising us. In Rio, you get into the groove without knowing it. People naturally turn into Cariocas. Put some Havaianas flip flops and sunglasses on and you're sorted.'

If you are to survive in Rio, never mind thrive, you need to have a very good instinct, and also to trust it implicitly. Most Cariocas believe in instant pleasure and living exclusively in the moment – not so much mindfulness as soulfulness. Kaiser certainly didn't worry about tomorrow. He rarely worried about later today. 'Kaiser is a typical Carioca – a chancer,' says his friend Júnior Negão, the beach footballer who won a record nine World Cups between 1995 and 2004. 'He's the kind of guy who wakes up not knowing whether he's going to eat in the best restaurant in town or go hungry. One day he won't have any shoes and the next he'll be dressed up to the nines at a fancy event.' In Rio, the default setting is hedonism, and everyone is having an all-life party.

\*\*\*

Kaiser signed his first youth contract with Botafogo a few months after his goal in the Father Christmas game at the Maracanã. His mum put two and two together and made 175, planning a future for the whole family on the assumption that Kaiser would become a superstar. She was a functioning alcoholic, and for years he had been forced to deliver homemade lunchboxes to earn extra money for her. He winces as he recalls soup and beans scalding his bare legs, and his mother beating him if he returned home with any of the money missing. 'She had suffered in life and she took it out on me,' he says. 'I'm not angry with her. She was just trying to get by.'

Kaiser adored his father almost as much as he feared his mother. 'He was super cool: intelligent, educated, classy, cultured, studious. He put a lot of value on culture. My mum was the complete opposite.' Kaiser's dad worked long hours as the manager of an elevator company and was oblivious to the fraught relationship between his wife and son. Kaiser concluded that, if his mum beat him up over a few missing cruzeiros, it probably wasn't safe to reveal her abuse and alcoholism.

Like many in those days, Kaiser's mother was uneducated; in 1970, according to the Brazilian Institute of Geography and Statistics, a third of Brazilians aged fifteen and over were classified as illiterate. Her constant nagging wore Kaiser down and started to drain his love of football. At one stage she demanded to know why he hadn't made it into the first team. He was eleven years old.

There was another reason for Kaiser's increasing apathy towards football; he had discovered girls.

\*\*\*

Kaiser was getting impatient. Most of his classmates had lost their virginity, and they wouldn't shut up about it. Kaiser was content that his reciprocal lies were convincing – nobody queried his stories after the Jairzinho picture – but he was still desperate to have sex. After all, he was nearly twelve years old.

The opportunity came during a party at a neighbouring favela. The girl who first made a man of Carlos Kaiser was a fifteen-year-old called Elisa, the niece of a family friend. The setting was not the stuff of Hollywood: it was ten o'clock in the morning when Kaiser and Elisa sneaked outside to find somewhere more intimate. Elisa led Kaiser by the hand until they found an alcove that was partially covered by a large sheet of corrugated metal. It would suffice.

For most of his first sexual experience, Kaiser was distracted by the cold kiss of concrete on his bare backside. It was initially an unwelcome intrusion – and then actually quite helpful, because it delayed the inevitable. At that stage Kaiser was, by his own admission, a workmanlike lover. 'The experience was practical and objective,' he says. 'I wanted to lose my virginity and move on to the next one. It's not something I'm particularly proud of. This all comes from the culture in which I was raised. When you come from a poor background in Brazil, you start trying to display your masculinity very early.'

\*\*\*

Even before he was a teenager Kaiser reached the conclusion that there were two types of people in this world: him and everybody else. Kaiser's circumstances made him self-sufficient and resourceful. Before he joined Botafogo, he earned pocket money by selling flowers at the gates of local cemeteries. Kaiser's angelic face and enterprising spirit pierced those undertaking a solemn ritual, and they were usually happy to pay a bit extra for a bunch of flowers. Kaiser even had a decent variety and could cater for different tastes.

There was a reason for that: he'd lifted them all from around the cemetery at the crack of dawn.

The scam was an early example of Kaiser's unusual initiative – and his love of *sacanagem*, a Portuguese word that broadly means mischief but can refer to anything from mickey-taking to depraved orgies. When Kaiser was younger, it often referred to his behaviour at school. He enjoyed some classes and had a particular interest in reading about health and fitness. But if the subject didn't interest him, he could be monumentally lazy.

In December 1975, Kaiser's mum gave him a backhanded incentive. If he didn't pass all his end-of-year exams his Christmas would be cancelled. No presents, no turkey, not even a cracker.

The thought of hours of extra studying revolted Kaiser on a practical and philosophical level. He did his exams but knew he had probably failed a couple. On the morning of the last day of term, when the results were due, Kaiser enlisted his friend Gustavo for a bit of the old *sacanagem*. They broke into the school at 5 a.m. and left a letter in the headmaster's office saying a bomb would go off at lunchtime. A few hours later, on the way to school, Kaiser found an *orelhão*, the name given to the outdoor public telephones that looked like gigantic motorcycle helmets. He called the local police station, dropped his voice as much as pre-puberty would allow, and calmly asserted that a bomb would go off at Pingo Guimaraes school later that day.

Kaiser walked to school as normal, and faked shock when he was told why everyone was being sent home. By the time the results came through in January, Kaiser had already had his Christmas and eaten it.

Later that year Kaiser was struggling in physics. He had a poor relationship with his teacher, Mr Fernandes, and could not have cared less about how to measure liquid density or the difference between diffraction and refraction. The long game – studying hard, sucking up to his teacher – had its drawbacks, so Kaiser devised a shortcut. He asked around and found out that Mr Fernandes was rumoured to be sleeping with one of his students. A few days later, Kaiser arranged a meeting after class.

'Carlos,' the teacher began, 'thanks for coming to see me. I really admire your initiative and I'm glad you've recognised the need to improve your grades. I'm sure we can sort somethi—'

'Shut up.'

'I beg your pardon?'

'I said shut up. Listen, I know what subjects you've been teaching Isabel after school and the last time I checked they weren't on the syllabus. If my grades don't improve straight away – and stay at a high level – you are going to lose your wife, your house and your job.'

His grades improved accordingly. Long before Kaiser graduated from school, he had a PhD in street life. 'In Rio, you had to be streetwise,' says Kaiser. 'You have to deal with so many things that you either become a scammer or a sucker. You eat or get eaten. I became very cunning and survived through guile and willpower. I had to fend for myself. You either become what I became or you become a loser.'

Kaiser grew up in a world where the end justified most means. *Jeitinho Brasileiro*, the little Brazilian way, has become a guiding principle for the disadvantaged majority in particular. It is a form of social vigilantism, which involves circumnavigating obstacles – poverty, bureaucracy, values – and finding a way of getting things done. The little Brazilian way ranges from the ingeniously creative to the indefensibly criminal. In a country of contradictions, it is usually a source of both pride and shame.

\*\*\*

When the Brazilian Ronaldo joined Internazionale of Milan from Barcelona for a world-record fee in 1997, it was inevitable he would take the symbolic No. 9 shirt. It had previously belonged to the Chilean striker Iván Zamorano, who found a way to maintain some ownership of his old shirt. He took the No. 18 shirt, but placed a small plus sign between the 1 and the 8. In his head, he was still No. 9.

Kaiser, who wore No. 9 for much of his career, might have employed a similar trick by having 1+7+1 on his back. One-seven-one is the number in the Brazilian penal code for forgers and scammers and has become part of the language: the full spectrum of conmen and rogues are known as 171s. And as with cops and bacteria, there are good 171s and bad 171s.

The endless philosophical debate over the line between good and bad was accidentally symbolised by the footballer Gerson. He famously smoked sixty cigarettes a day, a life-style that did not impinge upon his ability to score a belter in the later stages of the 1970 World Cup final. Later he became known for promoting Vila Rica cigarettes. Gerson celebrated the fact that they were cheaper than other brands and, in an advert that all but sent rancid smoke coming out of the TV, uttered a phrase that would become notorious: 'I like to get an advantage in everything.'

This became known as Gerson's Law, and was soon used to advocate and celebrate unethical behaviour. 'Gerson hates this story,' says the football journalist Martha Esteves, who had the dubious honour of being the only woman to write about the game during the 1980s. 'He doesn't like talking about this because it had a negative impact on his career and his life. Gerson – a nice, honest guy – had his name associated with misdemeanours and craftiness. The vast majority of us skip queues, jump red lights, give the policeman a little bribe, but I'm talking about the bad craftiness of Brazilians.'

The character of the loveable rogue has been entrenched in Brazilian folklore since the eighteenth century, when the indigenous peoples of the south passed round the story about Saci Pererê. Saci is a one-legged black man who smokes a pipe and wears a magic red cap that allows him to disappear whenever he wants – usually after wreaking all kinds of havoc. Saci drops flies in soup, turns loose nails so that they face upwards, sets animals loose and burns all the food. Though he can be seen as anything from mischievous to malicious, Saci is generally perceived as an adorable prankster. In the 1960s he was the lead character in a famous comic called *Turma do Pererê*. He even has his own annual celebration: 31 October is Saci Day.

Saci Pererê is a personification of *malandragem*, an extension of *Jeitinho Brasileiro*. The *malandro* is the anti-hero of Brazilian culture: he is work-shy, lazy, thinks only of instant pleasure, has little interest in long-term relationships and is an expert in deception. Without realising, Kaiser was being drawn towards the life of the *malandro*. Especially when, at the age of thirteen, both his parents died.

# CHAPTER 4

# THE ORPHAN

Kaiser's mother died from cirrhosis of the liver, the result of decades of alcoholism. Three months later, his father suffered a fatal heart attack. These days, Kaiser talks about the experience of losing both parents at the age of thirteen as if it was just another rite of passage. 'It was very painful for me, the death of my dad.'

He lived at the Botafogo training camp for a while before moving in with a couple of aunts. They worked as maids; the humble economy of their existence hardened Kaiser's resolve to build a better life. 'I wanted to be a footballer to make money,' he says, 'and eventually to get out of the dump that I lived in.'

Brazilian kids have always been desperate to reshape their life through football. Gonçalves, a tall, gregarious centre-back who played for Brazil in the 1998 World Cup, founded a football school in Rio during his playing days. 'It's tough to become a professional footballer in Brazil because there's so much competition,' he says. 'The disadvantaged classes view football as a way to change their whole family's life for the better. At the school I take in a lot of lads from the local favelas. The parents bring them along when they're seven or eight, already planning a career for these kids. The reality is that only twenty per cent of all professional players earn over double the minimum wage. But the media shows the luxury lifestyle of Neymar and the national team players and everyone falls for that.'

The journalist Martha Esteves estimates around 2 per cent of Brazilian footballers come from a middle-class background. The majority grow up in poverty, a list that includes all-time greats like Pelé, Ronaldo and Romário. Sometimes the route from poverty to stardom can be particularly circuitous. Dadá Maravilha, who was part of Brazil's 1970 World Cup-winning squad, had never played in an eleven-a-side match until he went to prison, where an officer persuaded him to use his prodigious leap – hitherto reserved for scaling walls – on the field. When he was released Dadá committed one last crime, robbing somebody so that he could buy a football, and went clean. He scored almost 600 goals in his career.

Dadá was one of thousands who changed their life through football. Bebeto grew up in Salvador with nine siblings; the first thing he did when he joined Flamengo was to buy a house for his mother. Not everyone deals with the change so well. Brazilian football is full of tragic stories of players who come from poverty and return there as soon as their careers are over. The most poignant tale is of the great Garrincha, who died a penniless alcoholic at the age of forty-nine.

'A lot of those players don't have anywhere to go in life nowadays,' says Kaiser. 'Football is different from the NBA where they have great players who also have degrees. Why can't it be the same in football? Where the players have another vocation? No. They think they're going to be footballers forever.'

Gonçalves nags those at his football school to study off the field. 'Many athletes reach a high social status during their careers,' he says. 'But they don't prepare for after their careers. And because most of the players don't progress very far academically they end up falling a long way in terms of the social status that they'd reached. They attain a certain standard of living which they're gradually forced to diminish because they have no academic qualifications or the possibility of finding another well-paid job which would allow them to maintain their current life-style. That's a philosophy that the clubs should instil right from the under-10s.'

\*\*\*

Kaiser was released by Botafogo at sixteen. He was forced out by the club president Charles Bole, who was gunning for him after a fallout earlier in the year. Macalezinho, the star player of the youth team and Kaiser's best friend at the club apart from Jairzinho, had been released because of personal problems. Kaiser told Bole what he thought of the decision, using language that did not entirely demonstrate the traditional deference shown by youth team players towards the club president. From that moment, his card was marked.

Kaiser was surprised by his reaction to the rejection. For reasons he couldn't entirely fathom, he'd been finding football increasingly unstimulating. His main concern was not about the damage to his football career but to his earning power. Football was still preferable to – and more lucrative than – real life.

At school he was friends with the sons of Dida, the youth team coach at Flamengo. Kaiser asked if they could arrange a trial for him. Flamengo were the biggest club in South America, perhaps the world. Like any self-respecting

Botafogo fan, Kaiser hated them, but he wasn't going to go hungry for his principles.

\*\*\*

Flamengo was founded in 1895, originally as a rowing club, with a view to attracting well-to-do females. It was not until 1911 that they branched out into football, when a number of unhappy players broke away from Fluminense. They won their first Campeonato Carioca three years later and eventually became recognised as the people's club, with huge fanbases all over Brazil.

Those who have played for Flamengo talk about the experience with a reverence that is almost eerie. 'The only way to get a real idea of what Flamengo represents is to experience it,' says Júnior, the great full-back and midfielder who has played more games for the club than anybody. 'It's an institution that raised me as a man and a professional. As a player and coach I spent almost half my life in it.'

The da Silva family can see Júnior's half a life and raise it. 'Flamengo,' says Wallace, 'is our life story.' He and his brother Valtinho started their careers at the club; their father Silva, who was part of Brazil's 1966 World Cup squad, top-scored in three of his four seasons with Flamengo. All three are now employed by the club as coaches, while other relatives have taken part in rowing, athletics, judo and basketball. It gives new meaning to the idea of a family club.

Silva is in his late seventies, and his eyes come alive when he is asked what it's like to wear the shirt. 'Kid, you don't even know. Not even the Brazilian national shirt has the same effect as the Flamengo one. That's why people say it's the "holy robe". I can't find the words to explain how huge Flamengo is.'

There may be no words, but there is a number. 'We represent forty million fans,' said the goalkeeper Diego Alves in 2017. Flamengo have more supporters than any other club in the world. That widely cited figure of forty million is a fifth of the population of Brazil and more than the entire population of Argentina. The fact they have generally played their home games at the Maracanã, the temple of world football, adds to the sense of Flamengo as a religious experience. The holy robe, their famous red and black shirt, is the most iconic in Brazilian club football.

Kaiser joined Flamengo just as they were about to enjoy the greatest period in their history. Between 1980 and 1983 they won three national titles, the first in the club's history, as well as a state championship, the Copa Libertadores and the Intercontinental Cup. That included a magical twenty-day period at the end of 1981 when they became, in chronological order, the champions of South

America, the champions of Rio and finally the champions of the world. 'The best football team I've ever seen play was Flamengo in 1981,' says the veteran journalist Renato Maurício Prado. 'I would go as far to say that if that Flamengo team played the great Barcelona side of Xavi, Iniesta and Messi, I don't know who'd win.'

The team was built around the J–Z axis. Nobody has played more games for Flamengo than Júnior; nobody has scored more goals for them than Zico. The exact totals are not easy to verify – Brazilian football has never had a particularly anal culture – but the official club site says Júnior played 876 games and Zico scored 508 goals. Júnior was a left-back for most of his career, though that position was just a basis for negotiation: he might be the first defender in world football to have had a free role.

Flamengo's triumph in the Copa Libertadores, the South American equivalent of the European Cup, included one notorious, chaotic match. They finished level with another Brazilian team, Atlético Mineiro, in the first group stage, which meant a playoff in Goiânia to see who would qualify. The match was played on a pitch that had been cut in a bizarre pattern, a two-tone mess of ovals inside rectangles that looked like the dance floor in a theme nightclub.

The referee José Roberto Wright – who would later become famous for booking England's Paul Gascoigne in the semi-final of Italia 90 – sent off four Mineiro players in the first thirty-three minutes for a range of offences, some pretty minor. The match was suspended for half an hour after a pitch invasion from fans and officials. When it resumed, the Mineiro keeper Leite went down with an injury. Wright told him to leave the field for treatment. Leite wouldn't, so Wright sent him off 'to put an end to all the clowning'. The game was abandoned, because Mineiro were down to six men, and Flamengo went through.

Flamengo eventually reached the two-legged final against Cobreloa of Chile. That finished level, and Flamengo won another playoff 2-1. There were five red cards in that, too: a couple for Flamengo and three for Cobreloa. The roll call of dismissed players included the Flamengo substitute Anselmo, who it seemed was specifically brought on to be sent off. His brief was to take out Soto, the Cobreloa player who had been scraping a sharp stone against the Flamengo players. Anselmo chinned Soto off the ball and ran. Soto chased him around the field until he was able to reciprocate the gesture. Both were sent off.

Flamengo won the Campeonato Carioca a fortnight later, and then went straight to Tokyo to play Liverpool, the champions of Europe. They won emphatically, 3-0, with all the goals in the first half. Each was created by Zico, who passed Liverpool to death.

Football was almost a different sport in the eighties – pitches were bumpy and GBH was usually only a yellow-card offence. It shouldn't have been possible for someone like Zico, who was 5ft 6ins and skinny, to succeed. 'I played against him several times for Liverpool, Sampdoria and Scotland but never laid a finger on him,' said the Liverpool midfielder Graeme Souness, who was one of the toughest players in the world. 'He's the only player I never actually managed to make physical contact with. He was far too bright and saw it coming.'

Zico is remembered as a playmaker of rare genius, yet his goal record was also spectacular: he scored over 500 for Flamengo and 48 for Brazil. 'Being the bow and the arrow came naturally to me,' he said. The arrow struck a record 333 times at the Maracanã Stadium. 'The Maracanã is magical,' he says. 'I became a symbol of the Maracanã and I'll carry that with me for the rest of my life. The press in other states in Brazil even made fun of me, saying I only played in the Maracanã. As if I was upset by that!'

Zico was the idol of millions, including a goofy kid called Ronaldo, Roberto Baggio and another up-and-coming attacker called Renato Gaúcho. He was Brazil's first great No. 10, an unusual player in a country best known for its explosive attackers or deeper playmakers like Gerson and Didi. Diego Maradona called him 'a director of games'. In style, he was more Dutch than Brazilian, an architect obsessed with the creation and exploitation of space; a schemer who solved puzzles before most players even recognised them. 'Have you been to the Maracanã?' says Edgar Pereira, a defender who played for Fluminense in the eighties. 'Have you been right in the top tier? You have a perfect panoramic view of the whole field. Well, Zico played like he had that view. He saw *everything*.'

\*\*\*

Kaiser was daydreaming during a youth team game when a violent tackle from one of his team-mates led to a free-for-all involving players on both sides. The teams did not have shirt numbers on their backs, and all the referee could see were a load of mullets and Flamengo shirts. He waved the red card at Kaiser, whose pleas that the wrong mullet had been fingered fell on deaf ears. Dida, the youth coach, made Kaiser apologise to the whole team the following day; Kaiser refused, pointing out that he hadn't committed the foul in the first place. After a week-long standoff, Kaiser was thrown out of Flamengo. He went on Radio Globo, the audio arm of Latin America's largest media group, to apologise to Júnior, who had been influential in bringing him to the club in the first place.

Although Kaiser was embarrassed and livid, there was an upside to the incident. It made him acutely aware of the power – and potential – of mistaken identity.

# CHAPTER 5

# THE SICKNOTE

The staff and players at Flamengo had sympathy with Kaiser, and he was allowed to continue training at the club even though he was no longer an official part of the youth team. He was determined to show Flamengo what they had lost. He also wanted to take action against Dida, the man who had sacked him. It was time to channel his inner Saci Pererê. Kaiser snipped the elastic in Dida's shorts, slipped *cachaça* (a spirit made from distilled sugarcane juice) in his water bottle and started spreading rumours that his sons were gay. Dida knew what Kaiser was up to; Kaiser knew Dida couldn't prove a thing.

A few weeks later Kaiser was included in a reserves training game in Gavea, which had been arranged so that the Mexican club Puebla could look at a potential signing, the forward Beijoca. Kaiser starred, scoring two goals in a performance of such vigour and dynamism as to surprise himself, never mind anyone else.

In 1979, scouting was not a sophisticated business. A whim was usually enough to push a deal through. The Puebla scouts were so taken with Kaiser that they recommended the club sign him instead of Beijoca. Soon he was on his way to Mexico. 'They had high expectations,' says Kaiser. 'It was the same everywhere. I was never a great player – but I looked like one. When I got off the plane it was as if they'd signed David Beckham. I had charisma, lustre, which is rare. You're either born with it or not.'

Kaiser's aunts told him scare stories about Mexico, that it was no place for a sixteen-year-old to go on his own. Most of them didn't go in one ear, never mind out the other. When Kaiser arrived in Puebla he had a sore thigh and suggested that it might be a good idea if he didn't train for the first few days. He noticed how readily the coaching staff accepted his self-certificate sick note. They didn't even ask him to do a fitness test.

While he was injured Kaiser started to explore Puebla. He brought hardly any belongings with him so would often wear his club kit, which led to many approaches in the street. Kaiser's Spanish was rudimentary and there was much awkward miming with fans and team-mates. The situation was not ideal, but it was something for others to address. If people wanted to talk to him, they could learn Portuguese.

Kaiser's enjoyment of his burgeoning fame grew in inverse proportion to his enthusiasm for the thing that made him famous. It's often assumed that all footballers have their dream job. Some just do it because they are good at it. 'I'd lost interest in football by the time I went to Mexico,' says Kaiser. 'I didn't want to play. The reason I was a footballer is because it gave me easier access to women. I wanted to live the glamour of football but I didn't want to live the routine. That was a chore for me. I see myself as a positive example, not a negative one.'

\*\*\*

As the ball was played forward, Kaiser curved his run in between the centre-back and left-back. He sprinted through on goal, faced up the goalkeeper, cocked his right leg ... and fell in a heap.

'Aaagh!' he screamed. 'Son of a fucking bitch!'

When his team-mates gathered round, Kaiser gritted his teeth and squealed that he had torn a muscle in his thigh. He slapped the ground repeatedly in frustration before being helped off the pitch and into the physio's room. It was his first day of training with Puebla.

There wasn't a thing wrong with Kaiser. In those days there was no MRI technology, so medical departments had no way of assessing muscle injuries. Ultrasound scans were useful but unreliable. The injured player's word was a more accurate guide. No footballer lied about being injured. The only problem for physios was those who were so desperate to play that they declared themselves fit when they were not.

Kaiser played on this assumption. His spell at Puebla provided the template for his fauxcation. He avoided playing by faking injury, usually something undetectable like a thigh or hamstring problem, and repeated the trick everywhere he went. It would be impossible now, because of the advances in technology and communication, but in the eighties word travelled very slowly, if it travelled at all, and few people had any idea that Kaiser was starring in his own version of *Groundhog Day*. 'I did anything not to play,' he says. 'I felt no obligation whatsoever to Puebla. I spent three years having them on.'

He spent most of those three years with an unlikely fashion accessory – a support bandage wrapped ostentatiously around his left thigh. Puebla were the first club to give Kaiser the full treatment: ice, injections, physio and a supply of anti-inflammatories that might as well have been Smarties. Nothing could cure his niggling thigh injury.

'This is the story of an anti-footballer,' says Kaiser. 'I'd like you to use that: an anti-footballer. I want to clarify that I was signed by these clubs but I never played for them. I was a footballer, not a football player. When people call me a liar it pisses me off because lying would be saying that I chested the ball down and scored from twenty-five yards. There aren't any stories like that. There are no lies. I wanted to live the off-the-field life so I had to be in the football industry. I gave up tons of cash. I could have been a trillionaire if I'd kept to all the contracts I'd signed. Everyone tried to get me to take it more seriously, but I didn't want to play football. Not even Jesus pleased everybody. Why would I?'

When Kaiser heard rumours that Puebla wanted to cancel his contract, he started dating the niece of the president to ensure he was kept on. It was an ingenious virtuous circle. The main reason she was going out with Kaiser was that he was a Puebla player, and the main reason he was still a Puebla player was that he was going out with her.

Kaiser's love of women intensified during his time in Mexico. He was happy to chat up anybody, anywhere, and took advantage of the language barrier to portray himself as shy and kooky, a Portuguese-speaking enigma from Rio. He had a string of casual relationships but was still shocked when, just after his seventeenth birthday, he was told he was to become a father. Parenthood terrified

Kaiser. 'I wasn't mentally ready,' he says. 'I didn't think I deserved to be anyone's father.' The mother, whom Kaiser had met during a trip to Mexico City, decided to have the baby on her own.

\*\*\*

After eight months of treating Kaiser's muscle injury, and with the supply of anti-inflammatories in Puebla at critically low levels, the coaching staff suggested he continue his rehabilitation at a club in Rio. He would then return to Mexico when he was ready to play. When the president queried the plan on account of Kaiser's relationship with his niece, Kaiser delivered a majestic monologue about how homesick he was, and how his aunt was extremely ill. The president gave Kaiser his blessing and paid for a first-class plane ticket.

Kaiser returned to live with his aunts, both of them in great health, and asked his friend Maurício if he could come along to training at America RJ, a small Rio club that had built a reputation as the neutrals' favourites. Kaiser spent most days sitting watching the players, telling stories and chatting up the women who liked to hang out at the training ground. He was starting to realise he had quite a mouth on him, and that he had the effortless ability to make people laugh or smile. One day he told a girl he was on a mid-season break at Puebla, where he was the league's leading scorer with twenty-seven goals in twenty-one games. He was almost surprised to hear the words come out of his mouth, but the girl's star-struck reaction – and her subsequent interest in him – made an impact on Kaiser. He was becoming aware that truth need not be an absolute concept, and started to play Chinese whispers in his own head.

There was not a huge amount of money in pretending to be a footballer. Kaiser's contracts tended to be short, sometimes minimum-wage, and most players did not earn that much in the 1980s anyway. Kaiser also struggled to save money for tomorrow, never mind the distant future. But he usually had enough to sustain himself, especially as each contract came with a healthy signing-on fee. Besides, what Kaiser really wanted was not cash but cachet.

It was around the same time that he started to pour more resources into a self-promotion campaign. At eighteen he became the de facto PR manager for Regine's, a nightclub underneath the Meridian hotel. He was given the role mainly because the owner was impressed by his status as the leading goalscorer in the Mexican league. Kaiser adapted his stories as necessary. If he thought he was talking to a woman who liked a bad boy, then he was in Rio after being banned for a month for punching a referee.

The ability to think on his feet was one of Kaiser's greatest strengths. But even he was struggling when he was having sex with a married woman and her husband arrived home. Kaiser ran onto the balcony, wearing only a nervous frown, and stood waiting. His mood wasn't improved when he saw an old lady in a nearby favela pointing him out to all and sundry. After a few minutes, the door opened and a giant of a man walked out. Kaiser quivered as 6ft 4ins of cuckolded masculinity looked him down and further down.

'What the fuck is going on here? Have you been with my wif—'

'Sir, please excuse me. I climbed up to your balcony from the flat downstairs. I was with Mrs Ortiz and her brother-in-law arrived. I had no idea she was married and I was terrified he would beat me. I'm only a kid, I didn't mean for this to happen.'

'Fuck off! You've been sleeping with my wife!'

'Sir, please, think about it. If I was with your wife, do you think I would be standing out here waiting for you to sort me out? I would have jumped up to the next balcony or to the one below. I know I've done something bad, but I'm not that stupid. I've never even met your wife.'

The husband considered Kaiser's story for a few seconds, then called his wife over. 'See,' he said. 'That's exactly why I don't like you going out with that whore downstairs.'

\*\*\*

Kaiser was at Puebla off and on – and having them on – for three years before he left the club and returned permanently to Brazil. 'The town was too small for my taste. Living in those places bores me. I'm completely urbanised. You get sick of the place, just like you get fed up of being at a club for so long. That goalkeeper Rogerio Ceni stayed at São Paulo for two hundred years. Good for him. He loves football and he loves São Paulo. Not in my case. I love myself. I want to feel good.'

\*\*\*

The only place Kaiser felt good was in Rio. He went back to America, the club, and idled around the training ground. Few people questioned him being there, especially as he was such good friends with the club's best player, the attacker Maurício. He also got on famously with the president, Francisco Cantizano, who loved Kaiser's mischievous wit – not to mention that he was invariably surrounded by beautiful women. Kaiser learned an important lesson from his fallout with Charles Bole at Botafogo. After that, he made sure he befriended the president wherever he went, and by whatever means necessary.

After a few months there were some murmurs of discontent about Kaiser's never-ending thigh injury. A couple of days later, Kaiser arrived at training armed with a detailed, official document explaining his injury: it was all linked to a dental problem, and Kaiser needed to undergo further tests to see if he was suffering from Charcot-Marie-Tooth disease, a rare neurological disorder. Cantizano and other senior figures concluded that it was too absurd not to be true. Even thirty-five years later, Kaiser remembers it well. 'Pure lies,' he says. 'I had a friend who was a dentist. He wrote it on official headed paper for me. My teeth were fine and so were my muscles.'

Kaiser was so unconsciously addicted to hamming up his imaginary injury that he encouraged the physios to try anything, no matter how unorthodox. They did. Kaiser was given regular injections of corticoid in his groin, which had little impact on his thigh but plenty on his stomach. The corticoid reacted and made him put on over two stone in six months. Even now, he gets annoyed when he remembers people laughing about it. 'It's one thing being fat from being fat,' he says. 'It's another from having to keep using corticoid.'

Kaiser eventually got another letter from his dentist, prohibiting the use of corticoid, and went on a demented weight-loss programme that consisted of little more than water and salad. Kaiser knew that, while he could fake most things about being a footballer, an athletic body was non-negotiable.

\*\*\*

Tele Santana walked wearily into the press conference. His Brazil team had just been knocked out of the World Cup after losing 3-2 to the eventual winners Italy in an epic match, and he knew what that meant for the coach: effigies, abuse, probably a P45. But first, a vicious interrogation from the media. Yet the moment Santana entered the room, 200 journalists from around the world gave him a standing ovation. They did it again when he left a few minutes later. It was recognition of one of the most stylish teams ever to play in the World Cup, and bittersweet validation of Santana's beliefs.

A few minutes earlier, in his own quiet way, Santana had done something similar to his team. He broke the dressing-room silence to tell them that, while on paper they had only reached the last twelve of the tournament, in reality they had achieved something far greater. 'The whole world was enchanted by you,' he said. 'Be aware of that.'

Santana was the last incurable romantic of Brazilian football. He coached the 1982 team, which left an indelible mark on the World Cup despite only reaching the second group stage, and returned to do something similar in 1986.

Brazil were so serious about winning the 1982 World Cup that Socrates, their bohemian captain, even gave up booze and cigarettes for the tournament. He said that he got as much pleasure from playing in that team as he would if he had won the tournament, and there was plenty of truth in that. But no matter how many philosophical lines he produced – 'those who seek victory are just conformists' was one such – his eyes told a more nuanced story. It was heartbreaking that Brazil did not win the World Cup: for Socrates, for almost everyone in the world who loved football. One Brazil fan committed suicide even before the Italy game had ended.

There is a good argument that they were the most exciting attacking team ever to play the game. They scored fourteen goals in five games, most of them so spectacular as to form a portfolio that most international teams couldn't match in their entire history. They played a lopsided, freestyle formation that might be best described as 2-7-1, and that 3-2 defeat to a more streetwise Italy – 'the day football died', said both Zico and Socrates – is arguably the greatest game in football history.

Between 1950 and 2010, Brazil won the World Cup in every decade but one: the 1980s. Yet it is remembered with the utmost fondness; a time when *Jogo Bonito* was a reality rather than a marketing slogan. 'It was the artists' decade,' says the journalist Renato Maurício Prado. 'Talent would decide things in the 1980s. Now fitness is the priority. Socrates wasn't an athlete. He would have no chance of being a player nowadays. Imagine! He used to smoke in the dressing room.'

It's a recurring complaint among older generations: that today's players are athletes first, footballers second. In the 1980s, technique was the only accepted currency. 'Before training we used to play piggy in the middle, where you have a circle of players with the ball and one or two players running after it,' says Bebeto, who emerged at Flamengo in that time. 'Each person could only touch it once. The ball couldn't stop. I had that drilled into my head. The older players would shout, "First time! First time! You can't control it in the penalty area!" You had to be seriously good to get in that Flamengo team. Pep Guardiola's Barcelona are the modern team that most resembles our generation.'

The comparisons between Santana and Guardiola are striking. 'He preached the concept of tiki-taka in the 1980s,' says Edgar Pereira. Both are revered for their approach, but it can be hard work making football look effortless. Like Guardiola, Santana was a strict coach addicted to the frustration of chasing perfection.

Although the 1982 team did not win the tournament, the way they played enhanced the status of Brazilian foot-ballers. After the relative tedium of the 1974 and 1978 World Cups, Brazil were again the sexiest, most glamorous team in the world – on and off the field. Roberto Falcão, the AS Roma midfielder who won the Silver Ball for the second-best player at the 1982 World Cup, even dated the original Bond girl Ursula Andress.

It was the perfect time for Kaiser to be making his way in the game – especially as he was about to befriend the most glamorous player of the lot.

# CHAPTER 6

# THE DOPPELGÄNGER

Unlike those who worked for a living, Kaiser looked forward to getting up on a Monday. Every week his alarm would rip him from his sleep at midday and he would set off towards Miguel Lemos Road. There was always a gathering of Rio's star footballers for a game of footvolley – a cross between football and volleyball – on Copacabana Beach. It was a stage for the players to show off their skills, and their bodies, to the general public; to flirt and sup tooth-tinglingly cold beers. For Kaiser, it was an unmissable chance to network and increase his profile.

He became part of the group through his friendships with players like Maurício. He rarely got his toes sandy and it became a running gag whether Kaiser would play.

Kaiser says his favourite film is *Catch Me If You Can*, the Steven Spielberg film about the famous con man Frank Abagnale. Kaiser's story was more *Play Me If You Can*, as a series of coaches and players took part in the futile endeavour of trying to get him to play football.

Kaiser usually strutted around the beach wearing nothing but a pair of Speedos – he usually bought them one size too small – and aviator shades. 'I always wore Speedos,' he says. 'With my beautiful legs, what else would I do?' In those days, dental-floss bikinis were the female equivalent of Speedos. Everywhere he looked, Kaiser saw tanned, toned flesh.

A chance meeting made Kaiser focus even more on his look. One week he was introduced to Renato Gaúcho, the most exciting young attacker in Brazil, who was in town for a game with his club Grêmio. It was the start of an enduring friendship. 'Renato Gaúcho,' says Kaiser now, 'is the most important person in my life.'

His official name was Renato Portaluppi. But as he was born in Porto Alegre, the state historically famous for its cowboys, he was known to all as Renato Gaúcho.

Renato is the superstar Europe never knew. He was one of the greatest Brazilian attackers of his generation, an explosive right-winger with a pioneering combination of athleticism and skill. But the fact he played only seven minutes at the World Cup – and had a disastrous spell at

Roma, the only time he left Brazil – meant he remained largely unknown overseas.

'He was as good as Cristiano Ronaldo, Lionel Messi, Neymar,' says Bebeto, who played with him at Flamengo. 'A great player with insane potential. He was so powerful that when he ran at you, you couldn't stop him. I've never seen a better crosser. He didn't cross it, he passed it. The only difference between Renato and Ronaldo or Messi is that he loved going out at night.'

A teenage Renato announced himself in the 1982 Campeonato Brasileiro final, when he destroyed Flamengo's great left-back Júnior. Flamengo won the match but Grêmio's runner-up spot was enough for a place in the Copa Libertadores. After the game, Renato Maurício Prado went into the Flamengo dressing room to interview Júnior. 'Who the fuck is that right-winger?' he asked. 'What the hell was that?'

The World Cup may have passed him by, but Renato still managed to become world champion. In 1983, at the age of twenty-one, he inspired Grêmio to win the Copa Libertadores and the Intercontinental Cup, the one-off match between the champions of Europe and South America. Both victories included legendary examples of his explosive ability. The first came in the second leg of the Libertadores final against Peñarol of Uruguay; with four-teen minutes remaining, the aggregate score was 2-2 and heading for a third match. (At that stage a penalty shoot-out was only used after a replay.) Renato was boxed in by the right touchline, with no decent options. So he created a new one: he scooped the ball up – just enough to get the necessary elevation, not so much that the defenders could get to him – and smashed a huge, booming cross to the far post, where César scored with a flying header. It was an outrageous piece of improvisation. César's goal turned out to be the winner.

Five months later, Grêmio met the European champions Hamburg in the Intercontinental Cup final in Tokyo. They won 2-1 after extra-time, with Renato scoring both goals. The first came after he twisted Holder Hieronymus inside out and belted a shot through Uli Stein; for the second, he dummied to shoot, came inside Michael Schrode and finished decisively with his left foot. Renato's role in Grêmio's greatest year means he is seen by many as the most important player in the club's history, high praise given their alumni include World Cup winners like Ronaldinho and Everaldo.

He didn't stay at Grêmio forever. In Brazil it was normal for superstars to move around, and Renato became a kind of journeyman idol. 'Star players get a free pass,' says the larger than life broadcaster and former Flamengo manager Washington Rodrigues. 'They transcend those rivalries because they are immediately accepted. He could go to

Flamengo and join Vasco da Gama ten minutes later and people would still be overjoyed because he's friendly and charismatic as well as being an incredible footballer.'

Renato was an atypical Brazilian attacker – tall, muscular and explosive. He played as a roaming winger with an unorthodox, almost rambling style, and usually with his socks round his ankles. He didn't always look elegant with the ball, and even his famous, brilliant first goal against Hamburg involves a fair degree of improvised stumbling. Yet there was usually method in his untidiness, and it came off far too often to be described as a fluke. He had a polygamous relationship with the sublime and the ridiculous, but at his best he was decisive and devastatingly effective.

'Renato Gaúcho is the perfect male specimen,' says Washington Rodrigues. 'Renato is an exception to the normal body type. He combines strength, skill and speed, which is extremely rare in a single player. And his greatest asset? He has the strength and guts of a Gaúcho and the swagger and cunning of a Carioca. He's a Cariucho.'

The paradox of Renato is that, though he was one of the stars of such a celebrated era, he also foreshadowed an unwelcome change in the DNA of Brazilian football. 'He represented the transition from the 1980s into the 2000s,' says Renato Maurício Prado. 'He was still a very skilful player but he was strong, too. As Nelson Rodrigues says, he was as healthy as a prize cow. But he was totally irresponsible. Renato's career could have been a lot better, even though it was already very successful. He was always going out. He was a real laugh.'

Renato boasted about his ability to burn the candle at both ends. 'If he went to bed at five in the morning he'd turn up for training at seven,' says Pica-pau, who became his adviser. 'He'd go home and sleep in the afternoon. He didn't drink that much. He'd have a beer but it would last an hour. He'd have ten small beers in a whole night. So he took it easy.'

He was the first sex symbol of Brazilian football, a man whose appeal went so far beyond the pitch that he is often retrospectively compared to David Beckham. He was constantly on non-football TV shows and became a style icon who could start trends without realising. The huge popularity of mirrored sunglasses in Rio in the mid-1980s could be traced back to a picture of Renato standing with a girl reflected in his shades.

Renato was almost too hunky to function. He was the kind of man who was constantly objectified by himself, never mind anyone else. Videos of him playing footvolley almost needed an adult classification: he would walk round in Speedos that looked excruciatingly tight, ostentatiously spraying his whole body with a hose between matches.

There had been other pop star players before, but none who received the kind of attention usually reserved for boy band members. 'When he tied his hair back,' says Kaiser with fraternal pride, 'he looked like Richard Gere.' That is one of many references to Renato that instantly evoke a particular decade. When people describe him now, they invariably use the most 1980s of words: heart-throb. 'He was like a soap-opera star and that appealed to young people, especially young girls,' says the famous TV presenter José Carlos Araújo.

Renato brought an element of the soap opera to football, too, particularly with pre-match interviews that were full of trash talk. He had an instinctive ability to tread the lines between playful and serious, not to mention confident and arrogant. His default look was a knowing half-smirk that could be taken any number of ways. It is said that Renato once met Pelé in a nightclub and announced that, for each of the 1,284 goals Pele had scored, Renato had a notch on the bedpost. A confused Pelé asked whether this was officially documented.

'Renato was a lad in the good sense of the word,' says Washington Rodrigues. 'He was relaxed, likeable, friendly, affable. But he was a ladies' man and that affected him negatively because the more conservative people in football distanced themselves from him.'

On Valentine's Day 1985, Renato broke off from a Brazil training session to give a TV interview. He declared that he, the party boy of Brazilian football, had finally found love. He looked straight into the camera, pulled some flowers into shot, threw them in the direction of the lens and quivered, 'I send this flower to my love.'

After a perfectly timed pause, two more flowers appeared. 'I'll send one to my other love, Karen.' At this point the camera cut away to reveal a never-ending bunch of flowers, more of which were soon being thrown towards the camera as Renato wiped away tears.

'For Maria, oh God!'

'For my love, Carlinha.'

'Monica, you're amazing, I'd never forget you.'

The names of the women were those of his team-mates' mothers. The video became so famous that in 2015 it was copied on Instagram by the Barcelona superstar Neymar.

\*\*\*

Renato and Kaiser hit it off straight away. 'We had a natural affection for each other,' says Kaiser. 'He identified a lot with me because his lifestyle is the same as mine. The only differences are that he's married, rich and famous, and I'm not. But we were both born in Porto Alegre, we enjoyed the same things, had the same sense of humour and were both womanisers. We were like brothers.'

Kaiser made sure they looked like brothers, too. He considered Renato's style, his status as a heart-throb, and decided to sell some false Gere. Over the next few months Kaiser became Renato's Mini-Me, copying his look – especially his luxurious mullet – and physical mannerisms. He even adopted Renato's personality, ramping up his one-liners and snappy attitude. It had the desired effect. 'My reign truly began from 1983 when I was compared to Renato,' says Kaiser. 'They called me Renato's clone. It was easy after that.'

As was often the case with Kaiser, he took an old phenomenon and gave it a fresh twist. It's one thing to copy somebody, quite another to become their best friend.

Renato finally got to live in Rio when he moved to Flamengo in 1987 where he was part of an offensively good team that included Bebeto, Zinho and his idol Zico. In his first season, he won the Brazilian Player of the Year award. 'I'd been coming here for four years whenever the national team convened,' he says. 'When I came to Rio I fell in love with it. It's the way people live here. Easy-going, relaxed, always up for a quick beer at the end of the day. It was amazing because as well as playing alongside Zico – my idol – in the Maracanã, I won the Player of the Season award. I play with Zico and I live in Rio de Janeiro. Is there anything better than that?'

The relatively monastic Zico and Renato were very different characters, yet they got on famously on and off the pitch. 'I love him,' says Zico. 'I've only good things to say about him. He was a real joker, great for the group. He would fool around and go out but he'd work harder than anybody at training. And he always delivered on the pitch.'

Yet Renato's extrovert, flirtatious nature was not to all tastes. The journalist Martha Esteves recalls her fury when she was sent to do an interview profile of Flamengo's new signing. 'I've never left an editorial meeting feeling so much anger,' she says. 'I had a real hostility towards him. I always had a deep dislike for ladies' men, for sexy cocky men. They really get my goat.'

She soon changed her mind. 'I went to his house. I snooped around in every single one of his wardrobes, with all those gaudy outfits that people had in the eighties: shoulder pads, things like that. He had so many clothes. He had a huge Speedo collection. I met his fiancée, too, Maristela. It was love at first sight – with her, not with him. It was at second sight with him. After chatting for half an hour, we became friends and I did his profile. He's an incredible person. And he was a super-important player for Flamengo, because of his charisma and talent. He's always been a very happy person. He's involved in a lot of social projects. Many people don't realise how good a person he is – he has a very good heart.

'History is not fair with him. There was a lot of prejudice – he was good-looking, flamboyant, a rebel, and people frowned upon that. Some people envied him, some people hated him. His rebel fame didn't work out well for him. If he was a nice boy like Bebeto he would be remembered in a different way.'

These days Renato is in his mid-fifties and a respected manager. In 2017 he led Grêmio to the Copa Libertadores, becoming the first Brazilian to win the tournament as player and manager. The victory in 1983 is one of the few old stories Renato is happy to revisit. 'When he became a father he started to change,' says Esteves. 'He had a girl. I joked with him and said, "You're going to pay for all your sins, Renato." He would say, "Don't talk about that. I'm sending her to a convent." I think it made him see the past differently. He has really softened. If you ask him about his womanising days he cuts you off. "No, I don't talk about that, I'm a different person." And he really is. He doesn't want to be stuck with that image of a twenty-something womaniser.'

\*\*\*

Kaiser's decision to befriend Renato, the dude-in-chief of Rio, was a political masterstroke. Those who were irritated by Kaiser's unearned swagger were not going to do much about it when Renato and his entourage were around. It was a template that served Kaiser well throughout his career – by making the right friends, he had unspoken immunity. 'Brazil is very violent but I've never been affected by that,' says Kaiser. 'I'm hated by a lot of people but they think twice about crossing me because I have all kinds of friendships. Good ones, bad ones. I respect everybody.'

As well as immunity, Kaiser's social circle gave him credibility and opportunity. 'I was friends with the greatest of the greatest,' he says. 'My friends were the greatest of my generation and the one before it.' This is not an idle boast. Kaiser's most famous friend was the man who captained Brazil's immortal 1970 side. Everyone in football knows the name of Carlos Alberto Torres. And the voice: he was an avuncular character with the rich, deep twang of a voiceover artist.

'I'm very surprised they were friends,' says Martha Esteves. 'I don't understand what kind of connection they could have had. I think Kaiser probably conquered his heart. He warmed to him, looked at him as a son. Carlos Alberto was so well regarded. Being friends with him would open so many doors.'

As Kaiser's network widened, doors started opening everywhere. The next allowed him to copy Renato in another way: by becoming world champion.

# CHAPTER 7

# THE WORLD CHAMPION

Kaiser won the Brazilian championship for the first time in 1984. He marginally missed out on qualification for a medal, having played no games, but he wasn't about to let this mundane detail get in the way of a good yarn. Especially as it involved him being at Fluminense, the aristocrats of Brazilian football.

He was spotted by the coach Carlos Alberto Parreira – who later coached Brazil to the World Cup in 1994 – during a kickabout near the Rodrigo de Freitas lagoon. Kaiser's network of contacts enabled him to find out when some kickabouts were being scouted, and he would perform accordingly. Parreira was sufficiently impressed to suggest that Kaiser come and train with the club.

For a few days, as he prepared for his first session at Fluminense, Kaiser worried that somebody might have heard about his injury problems at America. He even considered the nuclear option of playing football. The more he thought about it, the more he reasoned that nobody would know. Fluminense barely acknowledged the existence of a little club like America, and when they did it was only to look down their nose. The chances of them knowing about his spell there were almost non-existent. And he knew he could say what he liked about his time at Puebla. The last time he checked, there was no Mexican Football Yearbook on sale in Rio.

As he lined up for his first training session, Kaiser looked around at the great and good of Brazilian football. The squad included Romerito, the Paraguayan magician, and some of Brazil's best young players – in particular the dynamic left-sided pair of Branco and Tato. Even Kaiser accepted he was out of his depth, and after a few minutes of playing simple, low-risk passes, he performed his skit. Kaiser exploded into a sprint and instantly pulled up clutching his hamstring. 'My first injury since I was fifteen!' he pleaded to anyone who would listen. 'I've supported Fluminense all my life and this happens on my first day of training!'

It was a pack of lies – he was a Botafogo fan – but nobody knew that, and there was sufficient sympathy and goodwill towards Kaiser that he was encouraged to continue his rehabilitation at the club. All he wanted was to be associated with Fluminense, a club that was symbol of wealth and privilege. One of the founding members of the club was Arnaldo Guinle, a member of one of Brazil's richest families. Fluminense has always been a traditional club, with one of the world's most distinctive kits, an almost psychedelic mix of green and dark red stripes.

Their intense rivalry with Flamengo – the matches between the teams are known as the Fla–Flu derbies – stems from the inherent differences between them. Flamengo are seen as the team of the masses, dismissed by Fluminense fans as 'the favela team'; Fluminense are the haughty elite. 'Fuck Flamengo,' thought Kaiser, 'this is where I belong.' The club was based in the glamorous South Zone of Rio, a place where it was compulsory to flaunt status, beauty and much else besides.

Fluminense's title win in 1984 was only the second in their history, though they were regular winners of the state championship, the Campeonato Carioca. The structure of Brazilian football meant that teams competed for two major prizes every year: the Campeonato Brasileiro, the national championship, and the localised state championship – the Campeonato Carioca in Rio's case. The state championship was often, paradoxically, the more important to the supporters. The difficulties of travelling across

Brazil for away matches diluted the experience of following a team in the Campeonato Brasileiro, and meant that rivalries were nowhere near as intense as those between sides who played each other in Rio or São Paulo. There's no point having bragging rights over somebody if they are 200 miles away.

The system meant it was possible to have success and failure in the same season. Fluminense won three consecutive Campeonato Cariocas from 1983 to 1985, yet finished eighteenth in the national championship in 1983 and twenty-second in 1985. But in 1984 they won both competitions. The triumph was inspired by the signing of Romerito, who went on to win the South American Player of the Year award in 1985 ahead of Diego Maradona, Enzo Francescoli, Zico and others. He got on well with Kaiser, who was slowly building a dream team of friends who could help his cause around Rio, both in and out of football.

Kaiser ingratiated himself in any way possible, from the everyday to the extraordinary. He would run errands or set players up with women. When one of Fluminense's star players knocked somebody out in a nightclub, Kaiser took the rap. He was happy to do anything for his team-mates – partly out of simple goodwill, partly because he knew he could call in a favour down the line.

One of the things that made Kaiser so popular in dressing rooms was his effortless ability to lift the mood. 'He cheered everyone up,' says Bebeto, the star striker who later had a couple of spells with Kaiser at Vasco da Gama. 'The vibe, the atmosphere was fun. We liked him so much that we played along with his stories. After two or three months he would just vanish, and when he did everybody missed him. Then after about six months he would come back saying, "I've been at this club, I was in France, I was in Portugal." Nobody believed him, but then he would show us newspaper articles or club ID cards to prove it. After a while, he'd vanish again. Then I'd be watching TV and a club would be presenting a new player: "The new signing, Kaiser!"'

Kaiser usually joined clubs on an informal basis, with no contract, but he didn't care about that. 'He wanted to take photos of himself to facilitate his off-the-field activities,' says Maurício, who took Kaiser to America RJ. 'He didn't care about playing. He wanted to get a picture of himself that he could show the girls: "Look, I'm a footballer" or, "Training was really tough yesterday. I need a massage."'

Most of the time Kaiser disappeared of his own volition, either out of boredom or because he instinctively felt he might soon be exposed. 'I didn't complete one contract,' he says. 'I'd arrive at a new club and it would be a novelty for me. Novelty is always good. Are you going to tell me that being with a woman for ten years is the same as being with her for ten days? That's a lie. Hypocrisy.'

Fluminense was the last team to dump Kaiser. He was only training on an unofficial basis, and with no sign of him recovering from injury it was suggested he should leave and try again when he was fit to play. 'They found me out,' says Kaiser.

He didn't care as he already had what he wanted. Fluminense's name was on his CV, he had official club gear and ID, not to mention photos with some of the best players in Brazil. All could be used in evidence when he approached his next football club. Or his next nightclub.

\*\*\*

Kaiser would never forget his first time at Studio C, the exclusive nightclub under Hotel Othon Palace on Copacabana Beach. By entering with Branco and Tato, two of the stars of Fluminense's title-winning side, Kaiser gained entry, not only to the club, but also the VIP section. As he pulled back the velvet curtains, Kaiser entered his own fantasyland. He prided himself on his poker face and acting ability, but at that moment he was so overwhelmed that he would have told a million truths. All he could see was a collage of flesh, everyone wiggling their hips to the samba and bossa nova of Jorge Ben Jor. He fell in lust eighteen times in the first minute alone. Kaiser regarded himself as a confident, accomplished lover, but this was a different league. The whole place was formidably comfortable with its sexuality.

This was Kaiser's entry to the inner circle. He didn't want to live the dream; he wanted to live the depraved fantasy. And he never, ever wanted to go back to real life. The 1980s may have a dubious reputation in some cultures, but in Rio it was a golden age of nightlife. Once he adjusted to his new surroundings, and was sitting comfortably at the huge round table reserved for superstar footballers, Kaiser decided he might as well try to monetise his lust. 'I'll bet any of you a hundred cruzeiros I can get a date with any girl in here.'

'Fuck off, Kaiser!' scoffed Tato. 'For a start, you don't have a hundred cruzeiros, and there is no way you could pull half the people in here.'

After a rapid back and forth it was decided that Kaiser should woo a tall brunette who resembled Raquel Welch. Kaiser walked over, studiously ignoring the jeers of his friends, and announced himself. 'Hi, do you watch *Mesa Redonda*?'

'No, what's that?'

'It's a football show, on every week, where they show the goals from all the matches.'

'I'm not really a football fan, though my brother is mad about Flamengo. Why do you ask?'

'He likes Flamengo? Of all the coincidences! That is so weird.'

Kaiser smiled and shook his head wryly.

'I play for Flamengo! I was going to ask you if I could dedicate my next goal to you as I thought you had a different kind of beauty to everyone else in here. You remind me of Raquel Welch.'

'You are a footballer, really?'

'Yes, look, here's my card. I get a bit tired of people thinking I'm not a footballer – you see, so many people have copied my look and try to pass themselves off as me.'

'How long have you been at Flamengo?'

'Three years. I played for the national team at the World Cup in 1982. You *must* have seen that?'

The girl's name was Larissa, and she and Kaiser went on a couple of dates, where Kaiser spent his hundred cruzeiro winnings, before she suggested he meet the family. Most people are scared of meeting the mother and father. Kaiser was terrified of meeting the brother, who would know he had never played for Flamengo's first team. He made his excuses, citing an imminent move to Italian football.

Kaiser's persuasiveness with everyone from beautiful women to septuagenarian club presidents was legendary among the footballers of Rio. 'His chat was so good,' says Bebeto. 'He had it in spades off the field. He had a silver tongue. If you let him open his mouth, that would be it. He'd charm you. You couldn't avoid it.'

Kaiser had the gift of the gab, and it kept on giving. But he also knew the value of keeping his mouth shut. Many of his friends noted with surprise how polite and under-stated his chat-up technique could be. 'I'd say the right thing at the right time,' says Kaiser. 'I'd keep quiet when I needed to. My dad used to say man's greatest skill is listening.' He was eloquent, witty and swore so infrequently that, when he did so, it was a tell-tale sign that he was genuinely angry about something, or that he was in danger of being exposed.

There was nobody Kaiser would not approach. He had more front than Copacabana Beach. 'Even when he wasn't pretending to be me, he was always with beautiful women,' says Renato Gaúcho. 'Famous women, too. He was a sweet talker; upbeat and extrovert. What woman doesn't like a guy like that? And on top of that, they thought he was a rich footballer.'

\*\*\*

In a world where almost every Kaiser story is accompanied by a raised eyebrow or an unspoken question mark, every single interviewee talks about his sobriety in a matter-of-fact manner. 'Never,' says Fabinho, before switching to pidgin English to stress the point. 'No alcohol. No drugs. No cigar. Nothing.' Kaiser was equally monastic when it came to drugs and cigarettes. His only vices were women and Coke – Diet Coke, that is.

Kaiser may enjoy food but he has never touched alcohol. He attributes his hatred of alcohol to the excessive drinking of his mother. This is not to say alcohol had no use to Kaiser. He reversed the old alcoholic's trick by drinking water with ice in a nightclub, telling women it was vodka. And he was happy to show a certain moral flexibility when Maurício was asked to promote Dado beer. Kaiser went along for the ride and the freebies.

*** 

The 1980s probably had more fashion disasters per capita than any decade in history. In the South Zone, extremely low-cut tops were the norm – and that was just among the men. Some of Kaiser's old photos show him and his friends wearing gaudy, patterned shirts undone almost to the belly button. Then there were the trousers, often so tight that one false move would leave them urgently requiring the services of a tailor.

The men of Rio all subscribed to a fashion philosophy of uniform individuality. 'Everybody had the same style,' laughs Martha Esteves. 'It was ridiculous. Every guy would wear blazers with shoulder pads and really colourful, flowery shirts that looked like wrapping paper. It was all really standardised. Tight trousers with white trainers; sunglasses, always, no matter what time of day it was. It was really kitsch and really tacky. But back then it was cool.'

\*\*\*

In Kaiser's heyday, sex and football were inextricably linked. 'That's something that's been going on for a long time, especially with girls from poor neighbourhoods,' says Gonçalves. 'It's very common for the training grounds to be full of girls asking for autographs and trying to strike up a rapport with the players. It's all in the hope of a better life.'

The age of consent in Brazil is fourteen. 'We'd get to training and see girls in their uniform skipping school to hang out in the stands,' says Gonçalves. 'Either that or they'd come from the beach in their bikinis and towels to watch the training. There were days we couldn't focus on training because we kept looking over at tanned girls in swimsuits sitting in the stands. When we left there was a gauntlet of mums and daughters on one side and girls in their school uniform on the other.

'A lot of players actually met their wives at their clubs after training or in the Maracanã. It's natural. There was also a telephone in the changing room. So the girls would call the club telephone and asked to be transferred to the changing room. And whichever player picked up was like the fish who'd been caught.'

Gonçalves was catfished on one occasion, when he was seduced by the voice on the other end of the phone and agreed to meet that evening at an apartment in Tijuca. 'It was a neighbourhood with nice buildings, so I thought, "She must be hot". She spoke really nicely. I was imagining a beautiful blonde. I went up and when I rang the bell the door opens and it's the maid! I had a good look and said, "Are you Fulana?"

'"Yes, hi, Gonçalves. How are you?"

'"I came here to give you an autograph, sorry I couldn't bring a shirt. I have to be somewhere now. I didn't want to mess you around but I didn't have your number. I just had your address that I wrote down so I couldn't call you. Forgive me."'

Gonçalves made a quick exit, vowing never to answer the phone at Flamengo again.

\*\*\*

When he first started to explore the South Zone, Kaiser was still living with his aunts, which wasn't exactly conducive to all-night *pata-pata*. In Rio, there was a simple solution to that: the love motel. There was one on almost every corner, offering a practical, objective room to rent by the hour or by the night. The decor usually registered extremely high on the cheesometer, with round beds, mirrors on the ceiling and huge bath tubs. Kaiser loved them.

An adulterous culture is one of the main reasons for the success of love motels, though they are also very popular among young people who, in a fiercely Christian culture, are not allowed to bring partners home. Infidelity is rarely frowned upon either. 'You can be a womaniser and a great person in Brazil,' says Martha Esteves. 'It's so normal that we kind of separate the two.' It was common for footballers to go there from a nightclub, especially if they were married – or living with their aunt.

\*\*\*

Kaiser was getting sick of spending so much money on love motels and reasoned he might as well rent his own place. He needed extra cash for that, however, and had been unemployed since leaving Fluminense. Things were so desperate that he even took a real job at a solicitor's firm. He lasted until an infamous incident when staff kicked down the locked door of the communal bathroom to find Kaiser asleep. It was two o'clock in the afternoon. On his first day in the job. 'There was nothing for me to do,' says Kaiser by way of clarification, 'so I went to have a sleep.'

On another occasion he worked in a clothes shop that was owned by one of the directors of Vasco da Gama, and spent his days trying to chat up women in the mall while others earned his commission for him. He was also offered a job at a fish stall by a friend. Kaiser decided the smell of fish did not exactly complement the cologne he liked to splash on with abandon. He offered the job to somebody else, without telling his friend, in return for a favour.

For most of his adult life, Kaiser has had only one job consistently: being Carlos Kaiser. 'It was his way of life,' says Adriano Dias Oliveira, a friend of Kaiser's who played for Fluminense at youth level. 'His job was to fool people into thinking he was a professional footballer. He ate well. Got into the best places and parties. He dated women. And he would pretend to be whichever footballer was the man of the moment. He's a classic old-school Rio rogue.'

\*\*\*

The scale of Kaiser's con increased organically. His fake career perpetuated itself – the stronger his CV, the more chance of talking his way into another club, which in turn improved his CV. In July 1984, Grêmio were due to play the Argentinian team Independiente in the two-legged final of the Copa Libertadores. Kaiser knew the winners would play the European champions Liverpool in Tokyo a few months later, and he started to hatch a plan. He used his friendship with Renato Gaúcho to get tickets for the first leg in Rio Grande do Sul and organised a post-match party for the players of both sides. He befriended a number of the Independiente players, including the midfielder Jorge Burruchaga, who two years later would score the winning goal in the World Cup final, and arranged a threesome with two escorts for one of the directors.

When Independiente drew the second leg a few days later, giving them a 1-0 aggregate victory, Kaiser suddenly remembered he had been an Independiente fan as a child and decided he wanted to play for them. He contacted the director, who was sufficiently in Kaiser's debt that he pushed through a short-term contract for him. When asked by local media who he would compare himself to, Kaiser chuckled and replied: 'I'd probably say I have the same style as Renato Gaúcho.'

After temporarily relocating to Buenos Aires, Kaiser made himself popular in the usual ways and continued to arrange women for some of the directors. Football didn't really come into it. 'The team had thirty-odd players and I was among those thirty-odd players,' he says. 'I didn't play one game. I didn't kick one ball. I didn't score one goal. I told them I had a problem with the back of my thigh. They had to put another centre-forward in the team instead of me, a teenager called José Alberto Percudani. Don't ask me to lie and say that I played because I never played.'

Independiente also had a near namesake called Carlos Enrique, who proclaimed himself the best left-back in the world. He was known by his team-mates as 'The Mentalist'; and when he finally played for Argentina seven years later he was sent off in a Copa América match against Brazil after going so far over the top of the ball that he stamped on Márcio Bittencourt's back. Not the back of his leg; his back, right between the shoulder blades. There were five goals and five red cards in that match. Enrique had been sent off in a friendly against Brazil a few weeks earlier, too. His international career didn't last long.

After beating Grêmio in the Copa Libertadores final of 1984, when Enrique was in direct opposition to Kaiser's best friend, Renato Gaúcho, Independiente won the Intercontinental Cup with a 1-0 victory over the European champions Liverpool. The goal was scored by Percudani, Kaiser's replacement. 'I watched the game from the stands, I wasn't even on the team sheet,' says Kaiser. 'But I would say that I was a champion. It's like Ronaldo in 1994 and Kaká in 2002; they won the World Cup despite sitting on the bench. It made me happy because I came back to Brazil and everybody thought I was a world and Libertadores champion.'

Kaiser may have achieved the square root of bugger all on the pitch but at least, unlike some foreign players, he immersed himself in the local culture. 'I was there for a holiday. My life was the nightlife of Buenos Aires. There were eight hundred nightclubs. You can be sure I went to at least half of them. And, as always, the fact I was a player opened all the doors for me. I was there for a few months, not long. A city like Buenos Aires seems like an English city with educated, classy people. The illiteracy level in Argentina is zero. Great cafés. A really pleasant temperature for me being from the south of Brazil. There's no way you can't like Buenos Aires.'

It still wasn't Rio, though, and Kaiser was itching to return now that his reputation was further bolstered. He decided to try a new trick, one that proved useful throughout his career: a bit of grannycide. 'If I had to symbolically kill my grandma to not play, I would kill her. I would get a call saying my grandma died and I needed to return to Brazil immediately for her funeral.' That was how he left Independiente, two weeks after they had become world champions. His dear grandma would become the first human being to die on four separate occasions.

Kaiser had to alter his approach when he returned to Brazil. He was about to become involved with somebody whom nobody would dare try to con.

# CHAPTER 8

# THE PRODIGAL

Marco António is football royalty. He won fifty-two caps for Brazil and, at nineteen, was the youngest member of the immortal World Cup-winning squad of 1970. He started the quarter-final against Peru in that tournament, and later won five Rio state championships with Fluminense and Vasco da Gama. In the early 1980s, he was winding down his career at Bangu AC, a small club in the West Zone of Rio. A series of injuries kept him out for long periods, prompting whispers that his ailments were on the psychosomatic side – or that, in the parlance of the time, he was a lazy bugger.

This did not impress the club's patron and unofficial owner, Doctor Castor de Andrade. One day he walked over to Marco António, who was standing on the touch-line chatting to the players during training. Before António had chance to say, 'I used to play with Edson Arantes do Nascimento, you know', Castor whipped out a handgun and blasted some lead in the direction of his feet. It gave a whole new meaning to shooting the breeze. António jumped two feet in the air and then ran like Carl Lewis. 'See, you're fine,' cackled Castor. 'You can play the next game.'

He played the next game.

*** 

It was at Bangu, as teacher's pet of the most feared man in Rio de Janeiro, that Kaiser had the happiest years of his career. 'Bangu was all about Doctor Castor,' says Kaiser. 'It's just like before and after Christ. It was literally BC and AD: Before Castor and After Doctor.'

You should never judge a crook by his cover. Castor de Andrade looked like an eccentric, benevolent uncle. He was small and effervescent, with big, circular glasses and leathery features that broke easily into a playful smile. His charm, slightly camp charisma and philanthropy made him extremely popular, almost a romantic figure. 'Every person who worked with Castor only has good things to say, and the people who talk about him are all great people,' says

Ricardo Rocha, the former Real Madrid defender who won the World Cup with Brazil in 1994. 'It's not possible that Castor was not a cool guy.'

Yet it was common knowledge that he had been associated with hundreds of murders. When the TV presenter José Carlos Araújo was chatting to Castor and those allegations came up, Castor sought to put his mind at rest. 'He said to me, "Get this in your head: only people that deserve it get killed",' says Araujo. 'How was I supposed to interpret that?!'

In the 1980s, Castor was routinely described as the most dangerous man in Rio – a position that was not entirely without competition. He acquired his wealth and status through *Jogo do Bicho* (The Animal Game), an illegal bingo lottery that unwittingly changed football in Brazil. It all started with a financially challenged zoo. In 1892, with the Rio de Janeiro Zoological Gardens struggling to make ends meet, Baron João Batista Viana Drummond devised an idea to raise both money and publicity. Everybody who came to the zoo was given a picture with one of twenty-five animals on it. At the end of each day, a wheel was spun to select one of those animals. Those with the winning animal would take home a share of the money.

The game was so popular that it eventually expanded into city centres, where salesmen would walk around with signs or placards draped around their neck. A key part of its appeal was that, unlike state-operated lotteries, you could bet any amount you liked. Even Rudyard Kipling, on a trip to Rio in 1933, was captivated by the game he saw on every street corner.

*Jogo do Bicho* was made illegal in Rio in 1946. The government would have had more joy had they tried to outlaw sex. By then the game was so entrenched in the culture, and run by such powerful figures, that the authorities generally left it alone – or accepted bribes to turn a blind eye. There was a pyramid of salesmen, all the way up to the *bicheiros* – the crime bosses who earned millions from *Jogo do Bicho*.

That money wouldn't launder itself, which is where football came in. Castor was one of a number of *bicheiros* who used both carnival – the annual samba celebration that is probably the biggest party in the world – and football to legitimise their business practices. All of the main Rio clubs, with the exception of Flamengo, were run by *bicheiros*. It was a clever, calculated move that meant they could go about morally dubious pursuits with something close to impunity. It would take a brave policeman to try to arrest somebody who was adored by millions of supporters – and who, in some cases, had saved a club from financial ruin.

'The clubs were suffering and the *bicheiros* were their salvation,' says Claudio Café, one of the leading physical trainers in Brazilian football in the 1980s and 1990s. 'They fell from heaven. That model wouldn't work now, any-where in the world, but it was very important back then.'

In Brazil, there has often been a tolerance of corruption if it is seen to be for the greater good. A quote in the 1950s by the governor of São Paulo, Adhemar de Barros, has become embedded in the cultural consciousness: 'I rob, but I make things happen.'

Castor was a trained lawyer who inherited his father's business. It's hard to overstate how powerful he was. He had many of Rio's political elite on his payroll. He was also great friends with João Havelange, the president of Fifa. Most people cherish their disposable income; Castor had to come up with imaginative ways to dispose of his. 'He was drowning in money,' says Sergio Américo, who cov-ered Bangu for Radio Globo in those days. 'He was light-ing up cigars with $100 bills.'

Castor got plenty of Bangu for his buck. Officially he was just a patron of the club, but in reality he was in charge – not just of the club, but the region, too. The outsider status suited him perfectly. Bangu had always been on the mar-gins, even though they were the first team to host a profes-sional game in Brazil and the first to include black players.

'Doctor Castor is a god in the neighbourhood,' says Ado, one of the star players of Bangu's celebrated 1985 team. 'He was a father figure for everybody – the players, the fans and the neighbourhood residents. He would fight tooth and claw for the club and the area.' A father figure, and a Godfather figure. 'He was up against everybody in Rio de Janeiro: the government, the Brazilian police,' says Ado. 'He had to manipulate all of them to live well. And how did he do that? With charisma and money.'

*Castor* means beaver in Portuguese, and Bangu's shirt has a beaver in tribute. Everybody knew him as Doctor Castor, even if, technically, he had never enrolled in the Faculdades de Medicina at the University of Rio. All mafia bosses were called doctor, a gesture of submission that stems from Brazil's massive social gaps. In Castor's case, the name was not quite so excessive: in Brazil, lawyers are also usually referred to as doctors.

That doesn't mean the players lacked submissiveness. 'Everybody who played for Bangu under Doctor Castor was afraid of him,' says Romarinho, part of the Bangu youth team in the 1980s. 'A player would go onto the pitch shitting himself that if he messed up, Doctor Castor would confront him in the dressing room. He had a good side, too. If you played well or scored a goal, he would send you to a showroom and let you pick a car. But any player who said they weren't afraid of Doctor Castor would be lying.'

The players experienced a variation on Stockholm syndrome. Ado remembers the fear of walking into Castor's office, tiptoeing on eggshells, fearing that one innocuous move could lead to the eruption of a volcanic temper. On one occasion, two players – Rubens Feijão and poor old Marco António, who had already had his feet shot at by Castor – were late for training. Castor made them train naked. They weren't even allowed to wear shin pads.

The players would often kiss Castor's hand during training. In this case they were truly kissing the hand that fed them. He would routinely give money away to players, particularly those who were struggling. It could be anything: rent, medical treatment, helping out an extended family. 'All you had to do,' says Martha Esteves, 'was tell a sad story.'

At a time when many players around Rio were not paid as reliably as they might have hoped, Bangu's players received biweekly wages – and that was just the official salary. There were impromptu rewards, too, if somebody scored a goal during training. Castor arrived each day with a briefcase full of bonuses. The end of training was a free-for-all, in which even outsiders were allowed to play. Bebeto, a famous singer and Flamengo fan who shares a name with the World Cup-winning striker, often played with the reserves against the first team as training was winding down. He remembers two things in particular. That Castor would say, 'The singer can have some, too' while flinging money in his direction. And that Castor was always accompanied by Kaiser.

*\*\**

Elite clubs were often run like kickabouts: if somebody at the club vouched for you, you could often turn up and join in the training sessions. It was a verbal, informal culture in which things were taken on trust. 'Brazil is not big on facts,' wrote Alex Bellos in *Futebol: The Brazilian Way of Life*. 'It is a country built on stories, myths and Chinese whispers.'

Two of Kaiser's most reliable tricks were to arrive at a club with a recommendation from a star player, to give him credibility; and then to befriend the *bicheiro* in charge, to give him even greater immunity. The list of those who vouched for Kaiser included Tato, Maurício and Bebeto, all Brazilian internationals.

'Somebody must have come to the manager and said, "Sign this", because looking at the way he walks, you can see that he wasn't a footballer,' says Washington Rodrigues, the TV presenter who later became Flamengo manager. 'If I was the manager I'd ask him, "Run over there. That's all I need to see. You can go."'

The first time Kaiser met Castor to discuss signing a short-term contract, in early 1985, they were seduced by two women. As a man in his late fifties who was not entirely lacking in self-awareness, Castor was suspicious, but Kaiser reassured him that they liked him for who he was. The reality was that they liked him by the hour; Kaiser had set the whole thing up beforehand. It set the tone for an unlikely friendship in which both parties were happy not to scrutinise each other's moves too closely.

'Castor liked me because I wasn't afraid of speaking my mind to him,' says Kaiser. 'I wasn't scared of him; I treated him as an equal. He treated me like I was his son. If you're scared of Castor that's your problem. Those guys like rogues. They like cunning guys who are cheeky and tell it to them straight. That's how you deal with them.'

Over the next few years, Kaiser became a Bangu legend. 'He didn't play one game and he made history at the club,' says Ado, whose voice starts to go higher and higher until it reaches the universal pitch for incredulity. 'He became as important as any of the great players. For doing nothing! He never played! I don't think I ever saw him in football boots! I don't even know what shoe size he is! And Castor kept giving him contracts!'

Where others tiptoed on eggshells, Kaiser swaggered. He spent much of his time in Castor's office, a no-go zone with a direct door to the dressing room. Every day, before or after training, the players heard the lusty laughter of Castor and Kaiser. This was Kaiser's world, and he knew instinctively how to survive and thrive. He also knew that, to Castor or any of the *bicheiros*, his wages were peanuts – and well worth paying given his positive impact on club morale and their sex life.

'I was reckless,' he says. 'I had no sense of what I was doing. Castor gave me special treatment, everybody knows that. Nobody understood why, because I never lived up to expectations on the field. I know that in his heart I was the best. The fans might not have wanted me anymore but he did. What was I supposed to do?'

The journalist Renato Maurício Prado says that, in those days, Bangu 'was a complete madhouse'. The coach, Moises, was beaten up by a director in a row over the theft of a *Playboy* magazine, a bizarre and somewhat less gallant variation on the age-old story of two men fighting over a woman. And Castor's gun was used as a motivational tool on a number of occasions, particularly with injured players.

There were also suggestions that Castor was bribing referees, though nothing was ever proven. After one match, Castor and his henchmen chased a referee around the pitch. 'I saw who ordered them to attack me,' said the referee in a television interview, 'and it was the chairman, Castor de Andrade.' The players followed, hoofing the referee in an attempt to trip him up. Video footage showed a gun flapping in the back pocket of one of Castor's henchmen as he pursued the referee. When Team Castor caught up with the referee, he received a severe beating.

Castor had an alternative take on what had happened. 'I ran after the referee with a clear instruction saying,

'Don't leave the pitch! Wait on the pitch for the police!",' said Castor in a TV interview shortly afterwards. 'As I approached him shouting "Don't leave the pitch!", he might have thought I was trying to attack him, so he ran off. The footage shows the carnage but I didn't see anything.'

Castor had a variety of tools that he would use to persuade people to come around to his way of thinking. Sergio Américo recalls how Castor's heavies would appear in front of him, saying nothing, just as he was preparing for his daily broadcast on Radio Globo. The TV presenter José Carlos Araújo was with Castor when, after one late-night match, they arrived at a restaurant that had just closed. Five minutes later all the staff were back on duty preparing to serve the à la Castor menu.

One of his most powerful weapons was the whisper. The softer Castor's voice, the more the listener realised the importance of doing as he was advised. 'With the power he wielded over everything and everyone, he didn't need to shout at anybody,' says Kaiser. 'Nobody thought twice about crossing Castor because it wasn't worth it. A man like that didn't get fooled. He was sublime.'

When Kaiser joined Bangu he told Castor and everyone else that he was recovering from a muscle injury, which then became more complicated during his stay at the club. He'd told that lie so often that he was now doing it on auto-pilot, without a sliver of guilt. Kaiser was driven by con science, not conscience; he knew that here, as at his previous clubs, medical technology was not sufficiently advanced to prove or disprove his injury. Everyone believed him anyway. 'Kaiser was charming,' says Sergio Américo. 'We have a saying in Brazil: he was the kind of person who could sell a fridge to an Eskimo.'

There was only one problem for Kaiser. The closer he got to Castor, the more Castor wanted to see him play. 'He pressured me many times,' says Kaiser. 'Doctor Castor liked the way I was. He wanted to see my personality on the pitch.' As Marco António could testify, it wasn't wise to keep the Doctor waiting.

# CHAPTER 9

# THE MARKETER

Kaiser became an unofficial press officer at Bangu, long before the role existed anywhere else. Castor de Andrade encouraged Kaiser to deal with any media interest, and to promote the club at every opportunity. When the players asked why Kaiser was doing all the interviews, Castor would reply: 'Kaiser is the man.'

Kaiser was happy to promote Bangu, especially as it gave him the chance to promote himself at the same time. 'When Dr Castor got me to speak, to hold the shirt up, kiss the shirt, I would do it better than anybody,' he says. 'I became the team's marketing department. I raised Bangu's profile in the press. If you gave me one minute to talk, I'd talk for ten.'

He was an expert at answering the question he wanted to answer, rather than the one he had been asked. There was no angle that Kaiser could not bring back to the fact that he was a couple of weeks away from full fitness, and woe betide the defenders of Botafogo, Vasco, Fluminense and Flamengo when that happened. In a culture where the spoken word was gospel, and where journalism standards fluctuated wildly, Kaiser realised he could pass off almost anything as the truth.

A year earlier, during his short spell at America, Kaiser offered a junior reporter an exclusive interview with the club's star player Maurício – but only if he wrote a feature about Kaiser first. It was an extended interview profile that read like a press release. The first paragraph alone included a spectacular Kaiser hat-trick: that he was unable to play, that the club owed him loads of money – and, inside the first sentence, an entirely gratuitous reference to his romantic availability: 'Twenty-three years old and single, all Carlos Kaiser wants is to be allowed to play football.'

The article was full of gems that tiptoed perilously along the line between truth and fiction. America had rejected big offers for him from the English champions Everton and Paris Saint-Germain; during his spell at Puebla, he scored so many goals that the Mexican FA begged him to become a naturalised citizen and play for the national team. Then he complained about the impact of his treatment ('Due to the corticoids, I was really swollen and deformed, as if I was fat'); that the president of the club was not paying the players' wages ('but for his nights out, he'd open the club safe'); and that he had been suspended for a year as punishment for dating a granddaughter of a board member. The article ended in rousing fashion, and capital letters.

*'BUT HOLD ON, SUPPORTERS, I'LL BE BACK. THOSE WHO HAVE SEEN ME PLAY FOOTBALL KNOW I HAVE GOT IT.'*

\*\*\*

In the openness and occasional honesty of his interviews, Kaiser reflected the times. 'Footballers used to be more human, more normal,' says Renato Maurício Prado. 'You could call players like Zico and Júnior at home or go to their house for breakfast. Nowadays if you want to talk to a footballer you have to call about three hundred and twelve press agents and talk to the image rights guy and only then you might get a press conference interview.'

The fault lies not just with the players. The world was very different in the eighties: no saturation coverage, no clickbait, no camera phones, no culture of faux outrage. 'Nowadays the players see the press as their enemy,' says

Júnior. 'Back then you'd feel honoured if a journalist called you up for an exclusive interview. You'd go out for a beer and a chat with journalists and they wouldn't write something you'd said off the record. You felt like they were on your side. I'm still really good friends with some journalists from my era.'

It was a memorable, if challenging, time for Martha Esteves, who worked for the renowned weekly sport magazine *Placar*. She was in her early twenties, the only woman reporting on football, and routinely went into the dressing room after matches. Misogyny was so widespread in general life, never mind football, as to be almost mundane. Political correctness was a thing of the future.

'It was complete madness because the dressing room was really clammy and hot, and everyone would walk around naked,' she says. 'At first it was a bit of a shock but I was fine after that. It was full of journalists – a lot of *manja rola* ('dick-glancers') in there who just wanted to check the players' cocks because they were all naked. It smelt of feet and sweat. Nowadays it smells of Victoria's Secret because they're all so metrosexual.

'I remember one game at São Paulo in the 1990s when I went to interview Edmundo. He had a towel wrapped round him and was on this huge bench. I sat next to him, and in order to intimidate me he sat there with his dick out facing me. I kept interviewing him without looking down. I'm no dick-glancer! I always thought, "If I was a doctor I'd have to see naked men. I'm a journalist, so it's the same." I found it funny. I was so into that man's world that I forgot I was a woman. I was just a journalist like everyone else.

'The first big shock I had was when I watched a game sitting by the pitch, next to the radio journalists, and the supporters behind started chanting, "You whore! You whore! You whore!" We had things thrown at us – bags of orange peel, bags of piss. Not just me, all the journalists. I played deaf and blind. I looked straight ahead. "That's not me. I'm not a slut. They're not talking to me."

'Being a woman did open a lot of doors. Players and directors were a lot more friendly and accessible if they saw a young, keen girl. I wouldn't say they had a sexual interest, but they had a flirting interest. They wanted to be nice to me because I was this young, good-looking girl. I knew what was happening, but I would play the fool. I would take advantage of that and play the woman card. But some of the players were a lot more sexist than they are nowadays. They weren't very well educated. I knew that some of them were talking about me. When I arrived they were like, "Oooh look at the hot journalist, let's try to fuck her". It wasn't something that offended me. There have been players who've tried it on with me who regretted it. One player touched my ass and I slapped him. I don't want to mention his name. I told him to do one. He apologised and we made up afterwards. I always made my position clear from the beginning: "Listen. I'm a woman but I'm here to work. Treat me as a man, because if you do something I don't like I'm going to hit you." Zico and Júnior were the nicest to interview. They had a code where I would wait at the door of the dressing room and they would ensure everyone put a towel on before I came in. It's easier to remember the nice guys: Renato Gaúcho, Andrade from Flamengo. The Flamengo team in the 1980s were super-approachable. It got harder in the 1990s when the bad boys emerged full of attitude. Edmundo could be a very difficult person. He was super-arrogant. Within the clubs he never had many friends, and he really hated the press. During training sessions he would pretend to shoot at goal and try to hit the journalists, then laugh his head off if he hit them. He's a lot more accessible nowadays.'

Esteves recalls one particular row with Émerson Leão, the Palmeiras manager, who wouldn't let her into the changing room.

'You're not coming in.'

'Yes I am.'

'I'll call the bouncers.'

'You can call the bouncers, the governor and the fucking president, I'm still coming in.'

'Why do you want to come in, to see naked men?'

'No, I have a dick at home, and none of these dicks will embarrass me, so I'm coming in. This is Rio, this is the Maracanã, I'm working in my city, and you can go fuck yourself!'

Esteves laughs as she recalls the story. 'The whole dressing room was watching. I'm not sure I'd do that now. I was this crazy woman, I was doing my job. I walked in, I did my interview and I walked out.'

The interviews were usually worth the trouble. It was a time when players had not been media trained to within an inch of their personality. 'Football was easier and more exciting to work in, because you could get a thousand different stories,' she says. 'I liked to look at the characters and the human stories. The players didn't have that professional grooming they have nowadays. They were natural, they had charisma. There was a mythology to it as well. There were legendary players who would tell stories, who would create a character out of themselves.'

It was the perfect world for Kaiser to inhabit. By the mid-eighties he was so far in character that it was hard to tell where Carlos Henrique Raposo ended and Carlos Kaiser began. He certainly had the strut of a footballer. Eri Johnson, one of Brazil's most famous actors, will never forget when he met footballing royalty. 'The first time I saw Kaiser,' he says, 'he was crossing the street with such swagger that I thought, "That guy must be one of the best footballers in the world."'

As a big football fan, Johnson had no idea who Kaiser was. But the way Renato Gaúcho greeted Kaiser made Johnson think he was in the presence of someone different. 'I even regret not getting up back then. I apologise to Kaiser for that. I'd already met Pelé but I thought the way Kaiser walked was more distinguished. I should have got on my knees, because those legs were incredible!'

Kaiser studied the mannerisms, vernacular and attire of every footballer he met. He was like a boffin putting together the ultimate fake footballer – except he was also the boffin's subject. 'Man, he was like a celebrity,' says Maurício. 'He'd walk on the tips of his feet looking straight ahead: "Hey, buddy. I'm Carlos Kaiser, you have to respect me ... " He had a professional way of talking which was so convincing that people would be scared of him. It was as if he was Pelé or Carlos Alberto Torres.'

Kaiser's celebrity became a self-fulfilling parody. He had other tics, like bending his legs slightly as he walked. The most common was a caress of his luscious mullet, which he would flick forward insouciantly from behind his ears. In the 1980s, the mullet was the twentysomething male's weapon of choice. Kaiser's was, by any standards, quite spectacular: a luscious, wavy follicular statement of intent. 'His look was his trademark,' says Gutiérrez, one of the few non-footballers in Kaiser's social circle back then. Somebody else's trademark, sure, but let's not split hairs. And Kaiser's mullet was so majestic that it's a surprise he didn't have it insured. Three decades later, he says the favourite item of clothing he has ever owned is his hair. 'Life is marketing,' says Kaiser. 'I had the air of a star player. I knew how to talk and sell an image. People who saw me thought, "The guy's played in France, he's been at Flamengo and Fluminense, he's friends with Bebeto and Carlos Alberto. This guy is the real thing!" It's like Lionel Messi and David Beckham. Messi is a great player but the one who sells his image, products and everything is Beckham. Messi doesn't sell; he doesn't have the right way of talking. Carlos Kaiser does have it. I've appeared on several programmes in Brazil and I'm now attracting global attention. I don't think it was ever to do with my quality as a player or as a lover. It's because of my charisma.'

\*\*\*

As the clock moved past 3 a.m., Renato Gaúcho decided it was probably time to head into the town. The owner of one of Búzios's main nightclubs had invited him; although Renato did not fancy it earlier in the evening, he changed his mind as restlessness and boredom kicked in. He knew the club would not close until most people were getting up for work, and so he wandered over with a couple of friends, cutting through the queue to approach the door. Renato didn't queue or pay to get into nightclubs, so he was confused when a bouncer stepped across his path.

'Can I help?'

'The owner invited me along. I'm with a couple of friends. We came to have a look around the club.'

'But who are you?'

'I'm Renato Gaúcho.'

At this point the bouncer's face changed to an expression of insulted intelligence.

'Do you think I look like an idiot?'

'I don't understand.'

'You're not coming in because you can't fool me.'

'Fair enough, you don't have to know who I am but can you let the owner know I'm here?'

'You're not fooling me and I'm not calling the owner because Renato Gaúcho is already in there. I'm not an idiot.'

'Oh really? Renato Gaúcho is already inside?'

'Yes. He's in there now. You might look like him but you're not coming in.'

Renato was both intrigued and affronted and asked if he might be able to see this Renato Gaúcho. After five minutes of negotiation, the bouncer walked him inside and pointed to a table in the VIP section – where Kaiser was holding court with a group of women.

Renato smiled knowingly, turned on his heels and left. 'What,' he laughs three decades later, 'can I do with a guy like that?'

\*\*\*

Renato was amused rather than annoyed by Kaiser borrowing his identity. 'He was my Mini-Me,' he says. 'I started hearing all these stories: "This guy's slept with women pretending to be you, he's doing well out of your name." I said, "Whatever. If the guy's doing well, let him. Unless he's stealing or attacking somebody, let him do well out of it." He looked a lot like me. A hell of a lot. I would be at the team hotel the night before a game and people would say I had sneaked out and was with a woman. I had to explain that he was my double. I used to get in trouble at home with my wife. And it wasn't me. It was Kaiser. And not even that would make me stop being friends with him.'

At a time when players were not constantly on television or in newspapers, there were more than enough similarities – height, mullet, physique, mullet, swagger, mullet, sunglasses, mullet – to fool casual football fans, whether they were nightclub bouncers or desirable females. 'He styled his hair the same as Renato and if someone didn't know much about football they would fall for it,' says Alexandre Couto, who played with Kaiser at Ajaccio. 'He did well: 1-0 to him.'

There are tens, maybe hundreds, of women who will go to their graves convinced they have had sex with Renato Gaúcho. 'I used to go out with older women for money,' says Kaiser. 'When America or Bangu were playing away from home, there was somebody who arranged it. The women wanted to date Renato but they paid to sleep with Kaiser.'

There are stories of an up-and-coming footballer called Renato Kaiser, whose mother – so the legend goes – had a soft spot for both men and christened him accordingly. 'That's the first time I've heard that,' chuckles Renato. 'My technique and skill combined with Kaiser's sweet talk? Oh my God. I really want to meet this kid. He's going to be Superman.'

\*\*\*

Renato was not the only person whose identity Kaiser borrowed. He would claim the achievements of other players with a similar name, showing newspaper cuttings to convince people he was a star. Kaiser had a different mental checklist to most before a night out: keys, wallet, newspaper cuttings. And he rarely needed the wallet.

In September 1985, a young Grêmio defender called Henrique scored the winning goal for Brazil in the Under-20 World Cup final in the USSR. Kaiser passed that off as his own. Henrique had lighter skin and blond hair, but that didn't come across in match reports – especially as, with the tournament in the Soviet Union, most newspapers could not afford to send a photographer.

He also laminated articles about Henrique, the America striker, and took them around in his bumbag. He didn't even care whether the reports were heavily critical, just so long as they showed he was a player. 'The coach Vanderlei Luxemburgo took Carlos Henrique off for Carlos Alberto to give the attack more movement,' reads one of Kaiser's cuttings. Another gives him a 4/10 rating, saying he had 'no creativity and no purpose'.

Kaiser even managed to make a video of his greatest goals to impress women. He proudly boasted about one goal in particular, a bulldozing solo run by Vasco's Henrique against Flamengo in 1987. Henrique, like Kaiser, was tall, thin and bemulleted; on a grainy video, a non-football fan would never be able to tell them apart. But they would hear the commentary: 'GOL DE FANTASTICO! HENRIQUE!'

'I only ever saw him play on video,' says Valeria Gallo, an ex-girlfriend of Kaiser's. 'There was a very famous goal against Flamengo when he, how do you say it in football, resolved the game? He scored an amazing goal. Did you not know about that? I still have the video tape he gave me. It's worth its weight in gold because not even he has it anymore. It was him. I'm almost sure it was.'

# CHAPTER 10

# THE LOVER

The Bangu band provided a cheery soundtrack to every match played at the club's home ground, Moça Bonita. They went through a familiar playlist each time, with their most popular song taken from a children's TV show. 'Superfantastico' was the jaunty, squeaky anthem of the popular *Bãlao Mágico*, with lyrics like 'Superfantastic! The world is a lot more fun on the magic balloon! That's why I'm here!' All very innocent, except the balloon had the kind of evil face that tends to turn dreams into nightmares. At times the programme had the look of an eighteen-certificate kids show. There was another character which bore a striking resemblance to a dancing penis, and spent its time diligently stroking an egg. It didn't win many awards for subtle symbolism.

Castor loved the show, especially the theme, and got the Bangu band to trumpet it at every home game. 'Superfantastico' became a superstition: Castor was convinced Bangu would never lose a game if that song was played, and he wasn't going to let the times they *were* beaten get in the way of that belief. Whenever Castor gave team talks to the players, he told them they were the balloon bringing joy to an impoverished region.

He was not the only one who conducted the band. Kaiser invited them to play at training on Fridays, when they would sing: 'The world can cry and moan, but Kaiser is the best in the world.' The fact he had paid them to do so only partially compromises the touching sentiment, and Kaiser wells up as he sings the song almost thirty years later.

'Being back here is like being in a time machine,' says Kaiser, leaning forward in the dugout at Moça Bonita in an old Bangu shirt. 'If there's one place I lived with love and pleasure, it was here. I start to regret that I threw so many opportunities out of the window. I didn't reciprocate all the affection that people had for me. Not just the fans but the people who lived in the neighbourhood. The sexual conquests I had here, too. But we can't keep looking back into the past.'

When Castor heard the band singing repeatedly, and apparently unprompted, about an injured player it increased his affection for Kaiser – as did the sight and sound of random kids from the favela chanting his name during training. Castor assumed they must have seen Kaiser play elsewhere and started to think Bangu had the second coming of Pelé in their treatment room. They didn't chant with half as much zeal about Marinho and Ado, the star players of the team.

As with the Bangu band, Kaiser had offered certain incentives to lubricate their throats. In this case he told a young ballboy, Marcelo Henrique, to get the kids who were watching training to chant his name. In return Kaiser bought Henrique a bottle of Coca-Cola and a packet of biscuits.

Kaiser's relations with both the players and Castor were so good that he became a conduit between the two. The squad had long been unhappy at training during the day, when Bangu's forty-degree heat was at its most vicious, but none dared approach Castor about it. Kaiser, who by now was at the running stage of his rehabilitation, simply refused to train. When he was summoned to explain himself to Castor, he gave the Doctor the benefit of his football experience.

'When I was in Arabia, it was so hot that we trained in the evening. Come on, Doctor: forty degrees is subhuman. It's like the devil is training next to us. You're risking the athletes' safety.'

Castor concurred and changed the training times. Kaiser had never been to Arabia, though he had once seen a film about it.

When training sessions moved to the evening, Kaiser ensured they doubled up as a social event. He literally brought a busload of girls most evenings, organising a barbecue and a pool party during and after training. The club sauna became a de facto love motel. On one occasion, Kaiser arranged a samba band to perform during training; the session was watched by almost 2,000 people.

'I thought Kaiser was awesome,' says Romarinho, a younger member of the squad. 'He would always rock up with a van full of fifteen or twenty women. He'd be all nonchalant, like, "Hey lads, these are my acquaintances". Kaiser was the dog's bollocks. His contact list is ... immense.'

\*\*\*

Castor's investment enabled Bangu to develop a powerful side in the mid-1980s. It included Marinho, the flying winger who would follow the likes of Zico and Roberto Falcão as Brazilian Player of the Year, Mauro Galvao, Ado, Paulinho Criciuma and Arturzinho. And Marco António, the man whose dreams were still haunted by Castor pulling a gun on him.

Their finest season was in 1985, when they were runners-up in both the Campeonato Carioca and Campeonato Brasileiro. They came within a penalty shoot-out of winning the Brazilian national title, an achievement that would have registered extremely high on the Leicester Scale of Sporting Miracles.

The Brazilian championship has traditionally been the kind of thing you need a PhD to understand. In 1985 there were four groups in the first phase, with each playing two mini-leagues. The teams that finished top of each mini-league qualified for the next phase along with the two remaining teams with the best overall record.

Coritiba finished eighth out of ten in the first round, losing more than half their games, but finished top in the second phase – so although they were seventh in the overall qualification table they were one of four teams to go through to the second phase. They finished top of their group, then beat Atlético Mineiro in the semi-final to reach a final against Bangu.

The game at the Maracanã was effectively a home match for Bangu, with almost all of the 91,527 crowd supporting them. They had become the neutrals' darlings, with all of Rio captivated by the feelgood, age-old story of the plucky underdogs bankrolled by the most dangerous man in the state.

It was, and still is, the biggest game in Bangu's history. They were much the better team in a 1-1 draw. Coritiba's keeper Rafael was inspired, while Marinho had a fine goal disallowed for offside. Not only was it the wrong decision, it was a strangely belated one: Marinho had time to run through, go round the keeper, nutmeg the defender on the line and start a celebratory jig before the flag went up. 'The word "robbed" is very strong but it's the truth,' says Kaiser. 'We were shafted by the ref.'

It went to a penalty shoot-out to decide the league champions. Coritiba won 6-5. The identity of the fall guy was particularly cruel: Ado, who describes Bangu as 'the love of my life', had three spells at the club as a player and is now technical director. After he missed his sudden-death penalty against Coritiba, there was much nothing about Ado; a promising career never truly recovered from such a trauma.

That season Bangu won eight games more than Coritiba and had a goal difference of +32 to Coritiba's -2. But the book will always say that Coritiba were the champions, a feat that Bangu have still not achieved. 'Our biggest frustration is that we didn't bring Castor the title,' says Marinho. 'It wasn't our title, it was his title. The person most deserving of becoming Brazilian champion was him.'

Given Castor's history with referees, it's fair to assume Romualdo Arppi Filho also had a few sleepless nights over the next few weeks.

\*\*\*

Kaiser was in no mood for small talk. It was four o'clock on Sunday morning and he was working up a sweat at Caligula, one of his favourite nightclubs. He didn't want to chat to strangers — not about football, not about anything. Bangu had a big game later that day but that wasn't Kaiser's problem. He was a footballer, not a football player.

He was entertaining a new acquaintance in a secluded booth when he felt a tap on the shoulder. Kaiser snapped his head round impatiently, his face a picture of exasperated disdain, to see a nervous young man staring at him gormlessly. There was, he said, an urgent call for Kaiser.

Kaiser harrumphed his way to the office and picked up the phone.

'What?'

'It's Moises.'

'Fuck sake, Moises, what do you want? I'm in the beaver burrow!'

'The boss man wants you on the bench today.'

Moises was the Bangu coach. The boss man was Castor de Andrade.

'What? It's 4 a.m., I'm knackered. How am I going to play?'

'Calm down, Kaiser, you can just stay on the bench. I'm not going to put you on the pitch. But if the boss man wants you on the bench, you're going on the bench. I'm not risking my kneecaps because you're horny and having a late night.'

A drained Kaiser got back to the team hotel as the players were rising for breakfast. He went straight to bed. As word spread that Kaiser was going to make his debut, the players – who had no idea Kaiser had already ensured he would be a non-playing substitute – didn't know whether to laugh or cry. For months Castor had believed that Kaiser had a niggling injury that wouldn't go away. If it became apparent that Kaiser had been extremely economical with the truth, and taking money under false pretences, Castor was likely to want a lot more than a pound of flesh in return.

Kaiser played to the gallery in the dressing room, raucous laughter echoing as he outlined his plans to score a hat-trick and then head straight back to Caligula. The game started, and Kaiser was drifting happily into an al fresco siesta when the opposition took the lead. Three minutes later it was 2-0. Kaiser was furious, principally because the voluble discontent from the home fans was making it impossible for him to nod off. The punishing forty-degree heat did not help; Kaiser hadn't been drinking the night before – he never did – but he looked like a man with a furious Diet Coke hangover, sweat streaming into his sunken eyes.

In the stands, Castor had whipped himself into a state of murderous apoplexy. The match was only fifteen minutes old when he called for a walkie-talkie so that he could communicate with Moises on the bench.

'Moises, put the big man on. Stick him up front so that he scores.'

When Moises suggested that Kaiser was struggling with injury, Castor asserted that somebody else would be struggling with injury if his man wasn't brought on as substitute.

'Kaiser, the boss wants you on.'

'What?' said Kaiser. 'We agreed I wasn't going to play!'

'I've done my job. Go and do yours.'

Moises turned to Paulo Lumumba, the physio.

'Lumumba, warm him up over there!'

'For fuck's sake, Moises, you're taking the piss!'

As Kaiser started to warm up, he broke into a desperate sweat, caused by a combination of the heat and the fear that his first appearance for Bangu might be his last for anybody. Kaiser's warm-up was fast becoming a meltdown. If he wasn't scared of Castor de Andrade before, he was terrified now.

Like all self-respecting rogues of Rio de Janeiro, Kaiser had spent a life extricating himself from the malodorous stuff. This time, even he was struggling to see a way out.

# CHAPTER 11

# THE FIGHTER

Kaiser was on the verge of tears as he jogged in front of a section of home supporters who were unimpressed that he still hadn't kicked a ball for the club. The homophobic sleuths among them considered his luxurious mane and deduced he was a 'long-haired faggot'.

Kaiser couldn't remember the last time he threw a punch. But occasionally you have to compromise your principles to save your kneecaps – so Kaiser used the abuse from the stands as an excuse to clamber over a fence and into the crowd, where he started landing indiscriminate haymakers. A mass brawl broke out within seconds. It went on for so long that the match was stopped, with players on both sides watching from the sidelines.

Eventually Kaiser scrambled back over his fence, spitting blood at his feet. The referee sent Kaiser off before he'd had chance to come on the pitch. Kaiser went through the motions of protesting the decision, but inside he was doing cartwheels. He had escaped exposure, for the time being at least, and went to the dressing room to work out his next move.

\*\*\*

'Man, you are fucked.' Kaiser's heart thumped with fear as his team-mates returned to the dressing room at half-time. 'What have you done? The Doctor is going to kill you.' For once, nobody was sure of the extent of the metaphor. The chatter turned instantly to silence as Castor marched into the dressing room, flanked by two heavies whose knuckles seemed to be twitching in anticipation.

Without saying a word, Castor walked over and stood a couple of yards in front of Kaiser, who was sitting on one of the dressing-room benches. His eyes were at waist level, and the only thing he could concentrate on was the gun that was sticking out of Castor's pocket. Kaiser stood up and cleared his throat.

'Doctor, please, allow me to say something,' he said. 'God took both my parents away when I was thirteen years old but he gave me another father: you. When those bastard fans accused you of being a crook I lost it and went for them. They are not real Bangu fans. I should have taken all of those fuckers out. I know I let the club down but I would do it again. Don't worry, my contract is up in a week and I'll be off.'

Kaiser took a deep breath and waited. And. Time. Stood. Still.

Castor leaned forward and whispered in Kaiser's ear. 'You're a good boy, Kaiser.' And then he started cackling, the most beautiful cackle Kaiser had ever heard in his life. 'Joel!' said Castor to his supervisor. 'Put another six months on Kaiser's contract and double his pay. We need people like this at the club.'

Diet Coke and grilled chicken never tasted as good as they did that night. The story has become part of Rio football folklore. Ask anyone about Kaiser and it is one of the first things they will tell you. 'Kaiser spent another six months suckling the bosom!' laughs Gil, the former Brazil international who later managed Kaiser at Botafogo. 'Castor saw him as a son. He tolerated Kaiser's blunders and lies because he was a legend at the club.'

As on so many other occasions – when he was naked on the balcony, when Castor was seduced by those two young women – Kaiser employed one of the oldest tricks in the rogue's book. He told the person opposite him what they wanted, and needed, to hear. In this case, it may have saved his life.

# CHAPTER 12

# THE WORLD CUP STAR

Kaiser styled his hair like Elvis, unbuttoned his denim shirt to the breast and headed off to meet somebody special. Or, rather, somebodies special. The Brazil squad were at the Hotel Nacional, the cylindrical skyscraper designed by the famous modernist architect Oscar Niemeyer, for a pre-World Cup buffet with the media. Kaiser decided that having Brazil's greatest players in one room was too great an opportunity to miss.

When he reached the function room, Kaiser's entry was blocked by a security guard.

'Sorry, this is for the Brazil team and media only,' he said to Kaiser.

'Haha.'

'I'm sorry?'

'I said I admire your sense of humour.'

'I'm not sure what you mean, sir.'

'Oh, my G— You don't recognise me, do you?'

'Should I?'

'Well, I don't know, I suppose it depends if you are a football fan.'

'Not really, no.'

Kaiser sighed with weary disdain as he took an old Fluminense ID card out of his pocket. 'I'm Henrique, I play for Fluminense and I'm on the standby list for the World Cup squad. I respect that are doing your job but it would be pretty embarrassing if it got out that you had denied entry to a player of my stature. I wouldn't want you to lose your job over something like that.'

Kaiser pointed towards the left-back Branco. 'Look, ask him, he will confirm I'm not some chancer trying to con my way in.'

After a short conversation between the security guard and Branco, Kaiser was allowed in, accompanied by a thousand apologies. 'It's no bother,' he said. 'I understand you were just doing your job. But maybe next time you should educate yourself about the people you are supposed to be looking after. This isn't the Under-12s team.'

Once he was inside, Kaiser got photos with as many of the squad as possible – those he knew well, like Branco and Leandro, and those he didn't like Zico and Roberto Falcão. If any of the players queried him, Kaiser told them he was a senior editor at *O Globo*, Rio's biggest newspaper, and that he was collecting the photos to cheer up his nephew, who was in hospital having an operation.

Kaiser soon had his own personal collection of World Cup snaps with which to win favour with everyone from restaurant owners to women.

If he was asked why everyone else was in official Brazil gear and he was dressed casually, Kaiser explained that he had not had a chance to change into his sportswear as he had been late returning from a TV appearance that afternoon, delayed because he would rather sign every autograph request than leave one of his young fans unhappy.

*\*\*\**

The squad, excluding Kaiser, soon travelled to Toca da Raposa, the Cruzeiro training ground that was used as a base before they flew to Mexico. Strictly speaking, Castor de Andrade was not supposed to be part of their preparations. Tele Santana, the most disciplined of coaches, could barely believe it when, at the end of a training session, he saw the most feared man in Brazil conducting an impromptu penalty competition with one of his players.

Marinho, the star of Bangu's nearly men, had made his international debut in 1986 – a whopping ten years after playing for Brazil at the Montreal Olympics – and was part of an extended squad that had to be cut to twenty-two before the team went to Mexico.

Castor told Marinho they were going to have a penalty competition, with a crisp banknote the prize for every goal. It was not uncommon for Brazilian players to lark about during training. In 2002, the captain and key midfielder Emerson dislocated his shoulder while moonlighting in goal and missed the World Cup. As Marinho converted one penalty after another, Castor shouted, 'Hey, Tele, this guy is amazing at penalties, can't you let him play?!'

Marinho didn't make the World Cup squad.

\*\*\*

On the face of it, Brazil had almost the same personnel as in 1982. Santana was the coach, and their 22-man squad included Socrates, Zico, Júnior and Roberto Falcão. The flamboyant left-winger Eder would almost certainly have been in as well, had he not been sent off for chinning a Peru player during a friendly two months before the tournament. Yet the canary yellow was not quite as brilliant as it had been in Spain: all were in their thirties, most had injury problems, and only Júnior and Socrates were actually in the starting XI. Socrates later said the team were 'has-beens'. That's not such an insult when they had been arguably the greatest attacking team in the history of football, but it reflects the fact they were past their best.

The brightest new star was Careca, the twinkle-toed striker who had missed the 1982 World Cup through injury and would later excel alongside Diego Maradona at Napoli. There were also high hopes that the twenty-three-year-old Renato Gaúcho, who had been in blistering form for Grêmio, would make a significant impact at international level. He played in most friendlies before the tournament and was a shoo-in for the squad.

The team were at the Cruzeiro training camp in Belo Horizonte, a few days away from flying to Mexico, when Santana allowed them a night off to go to a barbecue. Four players missed curfew, but only two were caught – Renato and the defender Leandro. The others are still, more than three decades later, the subject of an *omertà*. Nobody is willing to give chapter and verse on what happened, though the majority say Renato was trying to help a monumentally drunk Leandro get back safely while the other two players jumped over a wall without being spotted.

Santana already had reservations about Renato's celebrity profile and chucked him out of the squad despite the pleas of the other players. Many felt Renato was sacrificed to scare the players into being on their best behaviour in Mexico.

The incident didn't just stop the press; it stopped the whole country. Martha Esteves says it was the story of the year. Kaiser read about it in the papers like everyone else and only spoke to Renato when he had returned to Porto Alegre. 'I didn't cry when my mum died,' he says, 'but I cried when Renato was axed in 1986.'

Leandro, a favourite from the 1982 squad, was given a last warning and kept in the squad. Renato's international career never quite recovered. He played forty-one times for Brazil and had his moments, including one divine slow-motion chip against Mexico during the Amistad Cup in Los Angeles in 1992, yet his World Cup career amounted to seven minutes as a substitute against Argentina in 1990.

Leandro, who was drinking heavily at the time, felt so guilty that he pulled out of the squad, and did not change his mind even when his long-time Flamengo team-mates Zico and Júnior drove hundreds of miles from the training camp to visit him. The absence of Leandro meant a last-minute call-up for Botafogo's uncapped right-back Josimar. He made his debut in the third group game against Northern Ireland and walloped an outrageous goal past the legendary goalkeeper Pat Jennings. In the next match, a 4-0 win over Poland in the last sixteen, he bettered that, rampaging past two defenders before screaming the ball into the net from a tight angle.

Josimar would not go on to achieve much more in the game but mention of his name provides a Proustian rush to those of a certain age in every football country in the world. He even has a magazine named after him in Norway. Along with Italy's Toto Schillaci four years later, Josimar embodies the magic and mystery of the World Cup before globalisation, when players who were completely unknown outside their own country captured the imagination of the whole world, and then often disappeared whence they came. Josimar and Schillaci are the World Cup's greatest one-hit wonders.

The 4-0 win over Poland put Brazil into their quarter-final with France with a record of four wins out of four, nine goals scored and none conceded. Their central-defensive pair of Júlio César and Edinho was probably the best in the world, the first time in history Brazil could make such a claim. They did not quite have the same attacking sparkle as the 1982 side, yet they were a much better all-round team, and are underrated in the pantheon of great Brazil sides.

Brazil could easily have won the tournament – and the mouth will forever water at what might have happened had they come up against Diego Maradona in the final – but lost in the quarter-finals to France on penalties after a classic 1-1 draw. Maybe Castor was right about taking Marinho for his penalty prowess after all.

The France match was almost perfect, a slow-slow-quick dance between two teams who, long before the term was invented, were disciples of tiki-taka. It was a cruel defeat for all kinds of reasons, not least because Zico, on as a substitute, missed a penalty in normal time that might have put Brazil through. Socrates then missed in the shoot-out. Neither would play for Brazil again. They never did win the World Cup, yet they were the brains of the last truly *Brazilian* team. 'Zico was so stigmatised by missing that penalty that, in Brazil, the 1982 and 1986 teams go in the same bag,' says Martha Esteves. 'It's almost like he wrecked that whole generation because he missed that penalty. It was very unfair.'

There is a perception among many that Brazilian football as we know it died in 1982, yet the 1986 side comprised the same players, the same coach and the same philosophy. It's just that the players were slightly past their magical best. They could still produce scintillating moments, both individually and collectively. Careca's goal against France was a delicious, rat-a-tat team move that showcased the unique Brazilian ability, honed during kickabouts, to play football in a space the size of a phone box.

'Nowadays football is all about perspiration,' sniffs Kaiser. 'In my day it was about inspiration. An example of a great Brazilian player now would be Neymar. My generation had over thirty or forty players of the same level. Players are more like athletes than footballers now.'

\*\*\*

Josimar could not cope with his new fame. He was seduced by a hat-trick of vices: women, booze and cocaine, the drug of choice for so many Brazilian footballers in the 1980s. 'He was a great guy,' says Gil, who managed him at Botafogo, 'but he was a nutter.' When he joined the Spanish club Sevilla, he brought his mistress with him and left his wife and child at home. Although he later played a part in Botafogo's celebrated 1989 season, his career never came close to touching the heights of Mexico. He won a modest sixteen caps, and by his early thirties he was winding down his career at Club Deportivo Jorge Wilstermann in Bolivia. His brother was shot dead in *Cidade de Deus*, the City of God.

Brazil's other full-back in Mexico, Branco, lasted longer at the highest level. He won seventy-two caps for Brazil and played in Italy for Brescia and Genoa, as well as Porto in Portugal and Middlesbrough in England. He went abroad for the first time after the Mexico World Cup, when he joined Brescia from Fluminense. He took the same flight to Europe as another Fluminense player, the young striker Fabio Barros, who was on his way to join the Corsican club Gazélec Ajaccio. It was the opportunity of a lifetime for both players – and for Kaiser.

# THE CORSICAN

The Wikipedia page on Brazilian expat footballers is never-ending. These days, almost all the best players leave well before they reach their peak. Neymar was twenty-one when he joined Barcelona; Gabriel Jesus and Gabriel Barbosa were nineteen when they went to Manchester City and Internazionale of Milan. In 2017, Real Madrid paid almost £38 million to secure the transfer of sixteen-year-old Vinícius Júnior. Brazil's 2014 World Cup squad included only four home-based players, and two of those were back-up goalkeepers.

The 1982 squad, by contrast, had only one over-seas-based player, and the 1986 squad two. A change occurred in the four-year cycle before the next World Cup, when Brazilian stars started to pop up all over Europe. By 1990, twelve of the twenty-two-man squad were playing abroad – and the other ten all did so at some stage in their careers. The brand of Brazilian football was so strong and glamorous that players became the must-have fashion accessory for any ambitious club, especially in Europe.

Fabio Barros, known to all by his nickname Fabinho, was one of those to move abroad when he joined the Corsican club Gazélec Ajaccio in 1986. His brother Marco stayed in his apartment while he was away and became friends with Kaiser during that time. When Fabinho returned to Rio during the French league's winter break, he started to hang out in the same group as his brother and Kaiser.

Fabinho and Kaiser got on straight away – they had a shared sense of humour, a youthful zest for life and a nerdy interest in football. Kaiser was fascinated that a player who was largely unknown in his own country could have become a star overseas, and constantly asked Fabinho what life was like at Ajaccio.

In January Fabinho returned to Corsica, and his performances in the No. 10 role were one of the main reasons that Ajaccio avoided relegation to the third division. The club owners speculated that Brazil must be full of untapped gems, and asked Fabinho if there were any players he would recommend. He promised to scout around when he returned to Rio for his summer holiday.

When he heard that Ajaccio wanted to sign another Brazilian, Kaiser was so excited he couldn't sit still. He was desperate to get away from Bangu before Castor de Andrade tried to get him on the pitch again. He nominated his services and impatiently dismissed any other suggestions made by the group:

'Romário? He's a one-season wonder.'

'How many times has Bebeto won the Intercontinental Cup?'

Fabinho had never seen Kaiser play, and suspected he wasn't good enough for Ajaccio, but he liked Kaiser so much that he decided to suggest the club should sign him. They were sceptical at first, so Kaiser offered to send a video of his best goals. He resented the cost of the airmail but figured it was worth the gamble.

A couple of months later, Kaiser – who still hadn't played a first-team game in his life – was off to Ajaccio. He arrived to find the club had planned a training session, a gesture he kiboshed by enthusiastically hoofing all the balls into the crowd. A bigger surprise to Kaiser was the warnings from his new team-mates that there was a strong mafia connection to the club, and that he should be careful.

'Mafia schmafia,' says Kaiser. 'I said, "Man, in my country I've already dealt with people a lot worse than them. And if they don't like me I'll get the first ticket out of here." I met these people and they liked me. The only thing that shocked me in Corsica was the climate. It was so cold that a penguin would sleep inside a fridge. People really like the idea of living in Europe. Not for me. I like the sun and the heat. The sun is pleasure. Apart from the cold, it was a piece of piss. The mafia didn't bother me at all. The most important thing I learned in Corsica is when somebody from the mafia said to me that Brazil lacked profession-alism, because drug dealers take drugs and whores have orgasms. I'll remember that for the rest of my life.'

\*\*\*

When a player joins a new club he usually receives a signing-on fee. Kaiser was given a signing-on female. 'A beautiful blonde escort,' he says wistfully. 'A gift from those influential people on the island.' It was Saturday night, a couple of days after Kaiser had arrived, and he could not find a vacant hotel for lust nor money. He grudgingly conceded that it probably wasn't appropriate to take an escort back to the presidential suite the club had put him in.

As he marched impatiently around Corsica, Kaiser wondered what kind of place didn't have any love motels. When they eventually found a motel after almost an hour, Kaiser was affronted to discover he had to pay for the room first – and that he couldn't just hire it by the hour like in the love motels of Rio.

The language barrier was such that Kaiser and his companion had only managed to converse in sign language. When they finally got to the room, she signalled that they could do anything except have sex, as she was on her period. 'You're having a laugh!' barked Kaiser in Portuguese. 'I've already paid and lost my money!'

After a fleeting yet monumental huff, Kaiser came up with a plan. 'I managed to mime to her: "I am a good sportsman, so when the pitch is flooded I shoot from behind the goal." You think I'd miss out after paying the motel? I'm Brazilian. I never give up.'

Kaiser vowed to learn the local dialect after his escort fiasco and had a working vocabulary within a couple of months. In that time he experienced something thoroughly distasteful in the Ajaccio dressing room: a high level of professionalism. 'Guy Calleja was a bad coach, really annoying, and the players were quite serious,' he says. 'They wanted to be in bed by midnight. Fabinho was ambitious, professional. Good for him.

'I had a lot of private parties with the directors and those other people. Corsica was boring, so we'd go to Paris, Lyon, Nice or Marseille. I used to chat people up in the perfume shops.'

\*\*\*

Fabinho and Kaiser were the start of a little Brazilian colony in Corsica. They were later joined by Renato Mendes Mota, a good friend of Kaiser and Fabinho's brother, and the young striker Alexandre Couto. Brazilian footballers are dotted around the world nowadays, but when the exodus started in the mid-eighties there were teething problems. For every Zico, who excelled at Udinese in Serie A and later became a kind of ambassador for football during his time in Japan, there were two or three Renato Gaúchos. He spent a disastrous season at Roma in 1988–9, when he failed to score a goal in twenty-three league games. He became a cult figure for how bad he was, and there are a number of lowlights compilations on YouTube.

Renato's lost season at Roma was a reminder that a happy player is an effective player. Although he explored as much of Rome's nightlife as he could, he was desperately homesick. 'I called him when he was in Rome and he was very sad,' says Martha Esteves. 'There was no footvolley, no family, no beach. He wasn't Renato.'

Nor did he find the most welcoming dressing room, with the local darlings Giuseppe Giannini and Bruno Conti making life difficult for him. The dressing room was only big enough for one heart-throb, and Giannini had taken the role. 'It was very political,' says Pica-pau, who remained Renato's adviser for much of his career. 'There were players who didn't like him because he was good-looking and attracted loads of women.' Kaiser comforted Renato by telling him he knew how it felt because he was having similar problems at Ajaccio.

Some of Kaiser's other friends also struggled overseas, including Gaúcho at Lecce in Italy, Tato at Elche in Spain, Maurício at Celta Vigo and, later on, Edmundo at Fiorentina. The strict professionalism was suffocating, particularly for those used to a freeform Carioca lifestyle. 'Brazilian footballers were never as professional as players in Europe,' says Gonçalves. 'We had a bohemian lifestyle, especially in Rio, with how easy it was to spend your free time at the beach or go to a samba show or a BBQ. There's not so much of it nowadays but that's how it was back then – especially at Flamengo. There would be famous Flamengo fans, singers and musicians in particular, in the dressing room. There would be a band playing. The final training session before a derby game was an event in itself. There was nothing professional about it.'

\*\*\*

Kaiser ended up getting more press than those who were actually playing for Ajaccio, most of it in the gossip columns. He was particularly close to Mancini, the sporting director. Mancini was an Italian in his early forties who ticked many midlife crisis boxes, including ownership of a Honda CBR 1000 motorbike. 'Mancini was really relaxed; playful, happy,' says Alexandre Couto. 'He liked to live well, let's put it like that. He never looked like a guy who carried a gun or anything, but you could see from the way he talked he was different. When he spoke seriously, there was something different there.

'Kaiser's relationship with the club couldn't have been worse. The coach and some of the players didn't like him. But Mancini had his back. It was like a wing of protection above Kaiser. The violence in Corsica can be really bad. Let's not beat about the bush, it's mafia.'

Kaiser became great friends with Mancini, just as he had with Castor de Andrade. 'I became a kind of Corsican ambassador. The people in the boardroom changed my name and called me Charles Henry because they wanted me to be a Corsican.'

Kaiser befriended some of the world stars who were playing in France, including the Colombian Carlos Valderrama and the Uruguayan Enzo Francescoli, who was the idol of a young Zinedine Zidane. When Zidane's first son was born in 1995, he named him Enzo in honour of his hero. Kaiser also met Ruud Gullit, one of the stars of the AC Milan side that won consecutive European Cups in 1989 and 1990, who took Kaiser to one of his favourite places in the world.

As a teenager, Kaiser had dreamed about playing for Ajax. They were the coolest club side in the world, with Johan

Cruyff inspiring a revolutionary form of Total Football. All of which had absolutely nothing to do with Kaiser wanting to play for them. 'My dream as a little boy wasn't to go to Disneyland, it was to go to Amsterdam, the land of mischief,' he says. 'What would I do at Disneyland? Go on the ghost train? Meet Mickey? That doesn't turn me on. I'd rather meet Mickey's wife!'

Most footballers who played in Rio in the 1980s and 1990s have heard a tale or twelve about Kaiser's time in France. 'What's the club he's talked about a thousand times?' says Alexandre Torres, the Brazilian international and son of Carlos Alberto. 'That's it, Ajaccio! The players used to gather round and he would tell stories. He created a fun, happy and light-hearted mood. He would tell stories and he would get players dreaming. That's why everybody liked him so much. When he told that story about the escort, all the lads went crazy! Everybody was jumping around as if it was a goal!'

The younger players were particularly wowed by Kaiser's tales. Roger Flores was seventeen, just another kid from a poor neighbourhood on Fluminense's books, when he spent New Year's Eve with Kaiser, Renato Gaúcho, Gonçalves and others. 'I was there with stars in my eyes as Kaiser told his stories. I thought, "Maybe this will happen in my life too." People like being around optimistic, funny people. That's what he brought to us.'

Some of the Ajaccio players were not quite as amused by Kaiser's stories. 'The team captain really hated me,' says Kaiser. 'He couldn't handle seeing me with so many beautiful women while he was stuck with his frumpy childhood sweetheart.'

Kaiser knew that the captain, a long-serving club legend, was campaigning for the club to get rid of him. He decided to do something about it.

# CHAPTER 14

# THE BLACKMAILER

Kaiser put on a solemn face and strained until a few tears started to dribble from his eyes. 'Look,' he said to the Ajaccio captain. 'I know I have been reckless and irresponsible. I come from a poor family in Rio and I got carried away with the temptations of this island. Give me another chance. You'll see a change straight away. If you don't, you can tell Guy Calleja, Mancini, whoever you like, to get rid of me.'

The captain told Kaiser he was happy to give him another opportunity, but that the team needed him to stop gallivanting, especially as they were battling to avoid relegation. The next day, the players were getting changed for training when they saw somebody out on the field practising free-kicks. 'Hang on,' said Fabinho. 'That's Kaiser.'

Kaiser had a reasonable game in training that day, especially for someone so patently lacking in match fitness, and there was fresh excitement that he would live up to his reputation. The winter break was imminent, and the management decided it would be premature to rush Kaiser into the team. They gave him a special fitness programme when he returned to Rio for the Christmas period, with a view to him finally making his debut when the league resumed in January.

Ajaccio drew their last game before the break, a decent result away at Gueugnon, and the players were in good spirits when they had their Christmas party at a local nightclub. Kaiser, who as usual was not drinking, noticed the players getting more boisterous by the hour. He became increasingly bored with their inane chatter and went off for a wander.

An hour or so later, Kaiser returned with a group of women, who joined the players' table. As the evening progressed, nature started to take its course and there were particularly lusty cheers from the players when their straight-laced captain disappeared with one of the ladies.

Fabinho and Kaiser were due to fly home the following day. Before that, the team met for a comedown lunch and debrief. The consensus was that it had been one of the better Christmas parties. Kaiser sat next to the team captain and held court majestically. When lunch eventually arrived, Kaiser leaned forward and whispered tenderly in the captain's ear: 'Listen, I have nothing to do with your life but don't get in my way. Otherwise your wife will find out that you slept with that girl last night. She was an escort, you stupid fool. You're not the big stud you think you are. You might be captain but I'm in charge here, so don't bring me down. If you want to keep your marriage and your kids, you'll keep your mouth shut. You're not a bad man, but I am, so don't get in my way.'

\*\*\*

Kaiser was keen to leave Ajaccio – he'd been there four months – but was only going to do so on his own terms. He returned to Brazil for Christmas to tell everyone about his explosive career in France. He knew there was no chance of anyone in Rio knowing anything about the minutiae of the French second division, so he let his imagination run riot. He had scored eighteen goals in fourteen games, was being watched by the French champions Bordeaux and had even been invited to present an award at the Cannes Film Festival.

He enjoyed the trappings of his increased fame so much that he didn't bother going back to Corsica after

Christmas. He cited a non-existent passport problem, and eventually persuaded a weary Ajaccio board to allow him to look for a loan deal in Rio. He made a virtue of that, too: Kaiser spun an alternative story in which he had been sent home for disciplinary reasons after going out too much, and said the club would not sell him for anything less than $2 million.

At other times it suited Kaiser to pretend his time in France had been a triumph, and that he'd bought his way out of his contract because he decided it was time to make his name at one of the Rio super-clubs. That was the story he told when he pitched up at Vasco da Gama looking for a trial. He got his friends Bebeto and Tato, two of the stars of Vasco's team, to recommend him to the president Eurico Miranda.

Kaiser decided he should at least wait until the second week before pretending to pull up lame, just in case somebody had heard about the player who was injured in his first training session at Fluminense a few years earlier. The problem was that, though he knew he was good enough to play for clubs like Bangu, America and Ajaccio, he also realised he was out of his depth at Vasco. To ensure he wasn't exposed, Kaiser developed a trick that would become familiar to those who played with him.

'He could go twenty-five to thirty minutes without touching the ball,' says Ricardo Rocha, the World

Cup-winning defender who played with Kaiser in some celebrity kickabouts. 'If the ball was on the right, he was on the left. If the ball was on the left, he was on the right. If it was in the middle, he was in defence. If the ball was in defence, he was in attack. He had a really bad relationship with the ball.'

One day, Ricardo Rocha broached the subject with Kaiser. 'I said to him, "Kaiser, you never get involved." He said, "Ricardo, I have a unique style of play. I play without the ball." He compared himself to Reinaldo, a brilliant player for Atlético Mineiro who was known for his off-the-ball movement. We would die laughing. He was a cheeky bugger.'

Ricardo Rocha played alongside Romário, Gheorghe Hagi, Ronaldo, Hugo Sánchez and others, so he knows what an icon looks like. 'Kaiser is one of the most iconic figures in world football,' he says. 'It's a unique story. He's a footballer who played without playing. Nobody else has remained in football without playing for as long as he did. He did so because of his human touch. Everybody liked Kaiser. He was amazing off the field. He ate well. He would tell jokes. He only had one problem: the ball.'

In theory, Kaiser was a centre-forward. In reality, he was a really false nine. 'I was a futuristic footballer,' he says enigmatically. 'I was years ahead of my time.'

Kaiser may not have done much on the pitch at Vasco, or indeed anything, but he did help the club win the title in 1989. Tato, the maverick winger, was having major personal problems during the season, with a crumbling marriage and widespread stories of alcohol and drug abuse. Kaiser became Tato's minder, his therapist, his wingman – and, in all probability, his pimp. Whatever he did, it worked.

'Tato had really serious personal issues, and Kaiser played a huge part in helping us rehabilitate that player,' says Paulo Angioni, who was the club's director of football at the time. 'Tato really liked him, too. And Kaiser had a really important function for us as well as that player, in helping him get out of the hole he found himself in. It was a very tricky situation.'

Tato had a fine domestic career, winning titles with Fluminense in 1984 and Vasco in 1989, yet he is another of his generation whose talent was not fulfilled. He played only three times for Brazil. 'He was a great, incisive winger,' says Sergio Américo, 'but there were always stories about his personal life which really damaged his career. The newspaper headlines weren't great: police raids, things relating to Tato's dark side. But as a player he went down in history, particularly at Fluminense.'

While he was at Vasco, Kaiser got the usual souvenirs. His CV now included the grand slam of Rio's clubs: Botafogo, Flamengo, Fluminense and Vasco. This was particularly useful when he was on a night out. 'There are some bad things about being a footballer,' says Roger Flores. 'Getting up early, training and pressure from the fans, especially if you are on the street after a defeat and some guy is giving you an evil stare and wanting to hit you. Kaiser just lived the good part, which was parties and being with hot women. Kaiser never lost. If Flamengo won he'd say he used to be a Flamengo player. If Fluminense lost then he'd never played for them. He was always at the party after a victory.'

\*\*\*

The game of the weekend had been a huge anticlimax. Vasco vs Flamengo, Romário vs Bebeto, was watched by a pitiful crowd and then curtailed because of floodlight failure. Afterwards the players of both sides went to Zoom nightclub for the *Garota Azul* ('blue girl') contest. Before it started, the nightclub owner wanted somebody to go on stage to talk about the Vasco fiasco. Romário and Bebeto, the two most exciting young forwards in Brazilian football, were in the building. Yet, almost inevitably, the man asked to talk about the game was Kaiser.

'What do you think about the lack of intensity in the stadium for such a big Brazilian derby game?'

'It's a farce. It's really shameful that this could occur in a country that wants to be considered the land of football. That's why I'm considering offers from Italy and Spain. Like my friend Pelé says, "This isn't a serious country".'

Romário, who was not always enamoured of Kaiser's tricks and fame, stomped around furiously demanding to know what was going on.

Renato Gaúcho recalls a similar incident in a nightclub in São Conrado. 'It was 3 a.m. and everybody was getting off with each other; beers, women, banter,' he says. 'Suddenly a guy grabs the microphone up at the front saying, "I'd like your attention because somebody is about to give a lecture about football." I thought, "Fuck! This guy interrupts the whole nightclub? There's a bunch of famous people here, none of whom would do that. Who is this clown?" They stopped the music and put the lights on the stage. And who comes on? Carlos Kaiser.'

On another occasion, three famous footballers were asked to judge a beauty contest. Jorginho and Gil, stars of the Seleção (the name given to the Brazilian national team, literally meaning selection), and you-know-who. Except he was introduced as Carlos Eduardo, the America player. Carlos Eduardo is black.

Kaiser knew how to steal the show. He also knew how to run it. 'He was the man in the biggest nightclubs of Rio,' says Alexandre Couto. 'A lot of them were exclusive clubs and he would be the one choosing who was allowed in or not. He was the Romário of Studio C.'

Kaiser was like a premium-line number, who players would call to find out where the best party was that night. For a while, they didn't even need to call him; they could just turn on the TV. Kaiser was going out with the presenter of *Bem Forte*, a sports show on CNT, and wangled a guest slot. As well as interviewing stars like Renato Gaúcho and Jairzinho, he would gratuitously advertise certain nights out in return for VIP treatment.

'The single guys back then would always seek him out,' says Fabinho. 'And he had options for all of them. Whatever they fancied. They might want to chill out in a nightclub. They might see a girl they're interested in. He had all the contacts to make things happen for those players. And that helped him further down the line when he needed something in return.'

Kaiser facilitated hook-ups all over Rio. 'I can't name any players because they're married,' says Kaiser. 'But it was a non-stop slut bonanza. Not like today where the guys leave traces. The players liked getting up to no good. Things happened and nobody found out. You don't want to know. Look, my thing is mischief. Every player has a million stories about me. But they can't tell stories that involve sex because they're married. They're not going to harm their own image, they're not going to expose themselves. The only one who's exposing themselves by telling the truth is me.'

* * *

Having completed the Rio grand slam, Kaiser decided to explore São Paulo's biggest club, Palmeiras. He used his friendship with Rocha, their midfield player, to arrange a deal. When Kaiser got there the club president was away, and no contracts could be signed in his absence. Kaiser was asked to trial for a week, without pay. The idea distressed him.

On his first day, before training, Kaiser spoke to a young left-back called Cacapo. Kaiser asked him what he earned per week and promised to double it if Cacapo slide-tackled him aggressively in the first minute. He did so, Kaiser pretended he had strained ligaments in his ankle and put his feet up until the president returned.

This time, it didn't go according to plan. A hardcore of Palmeiras fans, the kind of men dark alleys were afraid to have walk down them, found out about Kaiser's chequered appearance history. To this day, Kaiser has no idea who told them. They came to his hotel and warned him that, if he didn't leave São Paulo straight away, they would make absolutely sure he was unfit to play football. Kaiser took the next flight to Rio. He even paid for his own ticket.

# CHAPTER 15

# THE PIGGY IN THE MIDDLE

Even Kaiser accepted there were some battles he couldn't win. One was with the Palmeiras hardcore; another, though it was less likely to impact upon the contours of his kneecaps, was with Tele Santana. Kaiser fancied a return to the South Zone lifestyle of Rio but knew Santana, the romantic perfectionist who coached Brazil at the 1982 and 1986 World Cups and was now in charge at Fluminense, would not be thrilled with the idea of him joining the club on loan from Ajaccio. The two weren't entirely simpatico. Santana had worked with some of the greatest footballers of all time, including Zico, Socrates, Roberto Falcão and Careca. It's not hard to imagine his reaction if he ever saw Kaiser's first touch.

The suspicion was mutual. Kaiser had not forgiven Santana for chucking Renato Gaúcho out of the 1986 World Cup squad. He waited until August – when the Fluminense first team travelled to Holland for a mid-season break at the Feyenoord Tournament, a friendly event involving the hosts, Anderlecht and Benfica – before approaching the club. That allowed Kaiser to get his feet under the table before Santana had chance to point out that his technique was not entirely commensurate with established standards at Fluminense. He got Castor de Andrade to recommend him to the club's owner Farid Abrahão, a fellow *bicheiro* who was also president of the Beija-Flor samba school.

Marcio Meira, the club's head of fitness, turned up for work as normal on a Monday morning when a director asked him to take a look at a new player they had signed as back-up for the second half of the season. 'Kaiser was the first person I saw when I came into the dressing room,' says Meira. 'He had big hair, like Maradona, and sunglasses. He looked like he'd come straight from a nightclub! When he sauntered onto the pitch I thought, "What the hell is that?" Being a fitness coach, the first thing I looked at was his body. I thought, "It's going to be a bit of work to get him in shape to play." He told me he'd been injured for months.'

The absence of the first team teased Kaiser's ego. He suspected he'd stand out among the reserves and youth

squad and decided to put his boots back on. A few days'
training and then he'd get injured before the first team
returned.

He stood out all right. The day started with a game of
piggy in the middle, the usual way for Brazilians to flaunt
their ability and their masculinity. It was also the perfect
way to check out a new player, a kind of technical medical. Kaiser's first touch was imperfect: the ball clanged off
his shin and straight to the piggy in the middle, who thus
swapped places with Kaiser.

Over the next few minutes, Kaiser learned the true
meaning of the word futility: the players moved the ball
around with dizzying speed, and he could not get near
it. 'He must have been injured a long time!' chirped one
player. 'Go get it, Maradona!' said another. After a few
minutes Kaiser was on his haunches, gulping for a magical
hit of oxygen that might just save his life.

Meira, who was watching on with a combination of
bewilderment and pity, suggested Kaiser should do a
week's fitness training to get up to speed. 'I'll never forget
that day,' he says. 'It was so funny. He'd touched the ball
once and they had already nicknamed him Maradona. The
players are very welcoming. But they don't miss a chance
to take the piss.'

Kaiser didn't mind the ridicule. He was usually happy
for people to laugh with or at him so long as he got what

he wanted – in this case up-to-date Fluminense gear and the skeleton of a true story that he could manipulate as necessary.

'Characters like Kaiser are always well received in the football world,' says Paulo Angioni, who was the director of football at Vasco da Gama when Kaiser played there. 'We like upbeat people who you can tease without them getting upset. He's exactly that type of character. He has great qualities. He has kindness, generosity and joy.'

Marcelo Henrique, the Bangu ballboy who encouraged local kids to sing about Kaiser, was now part of the first-team squad at Fluminense. He could barely believe how easily Kaiser became part of such a prestigious club. 'To get to Fluminense I had to come through Bangu as a ballboy with loads of problems over there in the favela,' he says. 'Kaiser came along and signed without any problem. There's an old Pagode song: "What does he have? I don't have it". That's Kaiser. Whatever it is, he's got it. He signed with Vasco, Fluminense, Botafogo and Flamengo without kicking a ball. That should be in the *Guinness Book of Records*.'

Kaiser became popular with the Fluminense players, especially when they became aware of the breadth of his contacts book. He was starting to enjoy himself until the first team returned from Rotterdam. The following day, after training, the coach Santana called Kaiser over for a chat.

'Kaiser, I don't think you're going to make it at this club. You're not up to the standard we need to challenge for trophies. I know you are close with the president so we'll help you get your fitness back until you are ready to try out at another club. You can do all the fitness training you like with us, but you won't be involved when we do technical work. I'm sorry, I know I'm probably crushing your dream. The boys told me you've been a Fluminense fan all your life.'

Kaiser faked disappointment as best he could and thanked Santana for his candour. He was less sanguine when he found out that Santana had discouraged Marcelo Henrique from hanging out with him. From that moment on, Kaiser made sure there were two girls waiting for them at the end of each training session, largely to wind Santana up, and even persuaded Henrique to boycott a game against Flamengo at the Maracanã. Kaiser spent around four months doing fitness training before an opportunity arose to return to his boyhood club Botafogo. By the end of his time at Fluminense he was excelling in the physical work, especially the long-distance races. But he still wasn't allowed near the ball.

\*\*\*

While he was at Fluminense, Kaiser was the subject of a big feature in the newspaper *O Dia*, which included a rare picture of him in full kit from his time at Ajaccio. In the article Kaiser complained that he had been left in limbo by Ajaccio, who would not allow him to make a permanent move back to Brazil: 'He can't reach a financial agreement, nor will they sell him,' read the feature. 'The president of the French club commented to a sporting magazine: "I'll sell the whole team but not Charles".'

Kaiser also embellished the story of his spells abroad at Puebla ('We won the Mexican championship and they asked me to naturalise so that I could play for the national team') and Independiente. No longer was he in the crowd when they won the Intercontinental Cup against Liverpool in 1984. The language of the article was sufficiently ambiguous that the reader might reasonably think he had been on the pitch, maybe even played a part in the winning goal. 'Carlos Henrique, the poor boy from Rio, was there to lift the cup and be crowned world club champion. He returned to Brazil where there were parties, embraces, tears and emotions.'

The article also had the familiar, gratuitous reference to the fact Kaiser was single. All told, he could barely have written it better himself.

## CHAPTER 16

# THE PIMP

Gil flipped open his cigarette packet and sighed. He must have smoked the last one in his sleep again. He could not go without his morning cigarette, so walked down to reception to ask a porter to buy him some more. Gil was the Botafogo manager and the team, as usual, were staying in the Hotel São Francisco the night before a match. He was allowed to come and go as he pleased but wanted to show a bit of solidarity with the players, who were prohibited from leaving the building.

Gil was making small talk with the porter when a stretch limo pulled up outside. When the door opened, he was transfixed by a pair of stretch legs that emerged from the back seat. And when the rest of the body followed, Gil recognised one of Rio's most famous actresses.

He assumed there had been a mistake. Whenever Botafogo were staying, no other celebrity functions were allowed, to ensure the players were not distracted.

The actress said hello to the porter and walked towards one of the elevators. Gil was sufficiently intrigued that he ignored his increasingly rampant nicotine cravings and got in with her.

'Which floor?' he asked.

'Six, please.'

The sixth floor was where the Botafogo team were staying.

When they got out of the elevator, Gil loitered by his room door, pretending he couldn't find his key. The actress walked down the corridor and knocked on one of the doors. It opened and a bronzed hand slowly emerged.

'Oi!' said Gil.

Renato Gaúcho poked his head round the door.

'Oh, hey Gil!'

'Yeah, hey Gil. Send that lady downstairs, man.'

'Why?'

'What's she doing here? Do you want to have a nice chat with her?'

Renato walked into the corridor wearing a pair of yellow Y-fronts.

'Yeah, she just came to chat.'

'Nobody chats in their room this early in the morning. You can chat downstairs.'

A stand-up row ensued. 'I can't name the actress or I'll probably be taken to court,' says Gil. 'But she went nuts at me when I wouldn't let her in the room.'

When she eventually did go downstairs, Renato asked Gil if it might be possible to make a temporary alteration to the club's bonus structure.

'If I score two goals in the match today will she be allowed up before the next game?'

'Of course she will.'

Gil was lying; he just wanted a motivated Renato to score two goals. And he did, in a 4-0 win over America de Três Rios. Renato celebrated his second goal by holding up a finger on each hand in the direction of Gil on the Botafogo bench.

The players had no access to telephones when they were staying at a hotel before a match, so Gil knew Renato's meeting must have been arranged by an external source. He was approximately 100 per cent certain that person was Kaiser. 'He must have got the porter in on it as well,' laughs Gil. 'That bloke must have taken some money to let it happen. At 7.30 in the morning as well. He probably had morning wood.'

After the game, Gil banned Renato from seeing anyone in his room before Botafogo's next match. 'I told him, "If

I let you do it, I'll have to let thirty others do it. Hook up with her somewhere else." And it didn't happen. I was lucky I ran out of cigarettes.'

It wasn't entirely unprecedented for Kaiser to arrange sex for players. The difference at Botafogo was that he did it before games – and for the best part of five years.

*\*\**

It was normal for Brazilian players to spend the night before a match, even a home game, in a hotel. The culture of concentration – cocooning the players so that they could not get up to mischief – was well established. 'In Rio de Janeiro you can't trust the players at all because our culture is completely different,' says Gil. 'Europeans are more advanced than us. There's trust between the club and the player. Here it's all about samba, partying and women. And a bit of football. Give them an inch and they'll take a mile. Our culture doesn't allow for the player to stay at home. Otherwise he'll be having sex with his wife the whole night, go to bed late and when he turns up at the Maracanã the next day he's fucked.'

Kaiser helped the more amorous Botafogo players find a little Brazilian way around the frustrations of concentration. Gil found out years later that Renato's breakfast meeting was only half the story. The night before most games, Kaiser arranged clandestine orgies for half the first-team squad.

'Kaiser was with Botafogo for five years,' smirks Gil. 'We won two state championships and were runners-up in the Brazilian national league in that time. And Kaiser was there throughout, a legendary guy who made everybody laugh. Director, scout, whoremonger: he was everything you could think of, except a footballer. Most of all, he was the class pimp.'

The players were usually prohibited from leaving the hotel, with security guards often stationed on the door. Kaiser respected that. He would find out on which floor they were staying and prepare a party a couple of floors below. It would start after midnight, when the management team were all fast asleep.

'The players didn't need to go to the theme park,' says Kaiser. 'I would bring it to them. We filled our boots. There are serious players like Alexandre Torres and Bebeto but all the rest played for Kaiser FC. I think KFC in the USA was named after me.'

When Kaiser is asked whether the women involved were escorts, he turns his nose up with disdain. 'Don't insult them,' he says. 'They were artists, not prostitutes.'

It became a secret part of the team's pre-match routine. Kaiser was flown to away games a day or two ahead of the team; if any directors or management queried his presence, the players would explain that he was a natural comedian and storyteller who lightened the mood before games. 'Kaiser had the same kit as all the players, so as far as the public were concerned he was a Botafogo player,' says Gil. 'He had to present himself as a footballer or he wouldn't get anywhere.'

Gil liked having Kaiser around and did not question his presence, though he was unaware of the extent of his influence. 'If it had got out to the press,' says Gil, 'it would have been a global scandal.' Just in case any of the management team did find out, Kaiser added a layer of protection: he invited the club owner to the orgies.

Kaiser had been recommended to Botafogo by Castor de Andrade; he was great friends with the club patron Emil Pinheiro, another of Rio's most powerful *bicheiros*. As Emil was in his sixties, a man with unsated primal urges, it's likely Castor's recommendation had more to do with off-field matters.

Emil and Kaiser got along famously, and each gave the other what they needed. 'We knew that Kaiser arranged women for Emil but we didn't know that he was taking backhanders in return,' says Gil. 'Kaiser, the bon viveur, was receiving extra money and we weren't.' For the majority of his time at Botafogo, Kaiser was paid more than half the first-team squad.

\*\*\*

The roles of pimp and babysitter do not usually go together. In Kaiser's weird and wonderful world, however, they vied for prominence. 'I was basically a minder,' he says. 'I was at clubs to take care of the players' lives and make sure nothing bad happened to them. I was a footballer nanny.'

Kaiser was one of the first player-liaison officers and sorted anything from errands to restaurant reservations to those illicit five-a-sides at the team hotel. 'He would do everything,' says Bebeto, the World Cup-winning striker who was with Kaiser at Flamengo and Vasco da Gama. 'Whatever you needed, Kaiser would say, "Hang on, hang on. I'll sort that out for you." It was never a bad time for Kaiser. That's why I say he's a good guy. He doesn't hurt anybody and he's got a big heart. If you have a problem and he can solve it, he will. A guy like that can't be bad. So when he asks for something, what are you going to do? You're going to pay him back. Those friendships are eternal.'

There were times when Kaiser was a life coach to players, like Tato at Vasco da Gama. Some of his advice would not be found in most self-help bestsellers – 'Chapter 7: The Life-changing Magic of the Orgy' – but it was well-meaning and invariably effective. And though Kaiser was obsessed with sex, he did encourage players to resist most vices. 'You want to drink fifty beers and play the next day?' he says. 'Well done. Why not just have ten? I told them to calm it down. Nowadays there are a lot of scroungers around footballers. Useless bullshit advisers. I wasn't a scrounger. I was somebody within football who hung out with other footballers.'

The fact that Kaiser didn't drink made people trust him even more on nights out. He would drive them home, take the blame if they got into trouble or keep an eye on them if they were monumentally drunk. He also organised a variety of parties, from pre-match orgies at the team hotel to post-match orgies at country houses. And not just at Botafogo: Kaiser organised sex parties for the players at Vasco, Fluminense and Bangu, as well as for the directors at Ajaccio.

The players had a familiar weekend routine. They would have concentration on a Saturday night, with games sched- uled for late afternoon on the Sunday. There was usually a game at the Maracanã, and Kaiser would be waiting after the match to inform the players of the plans for the evening. They would go home to change and then start a long, lost night that would often carry on past midnight. 'The play- ers' party started when the final whistle went on a Sunday,' says Kaiser, 'and it finished when training started at 2 p.m. on Tuesday.' As Kaiser did not have to prepare for matches, the party started even earlier. 'My weekend,' he says, 'was Thursday to Tuesday.' He didn't like Wednesdays.

The Sunday night usually started at the trendy steak- house Porcão, where players from all Rio clubs would sit together at an enormous table, chewing the fat about the afternoon matches. Kaiser was invariably in the middle, cheerily signing autographs for fans. Later in his career, Renato Gaúcho was sponsored by the restaurant and brazenly wore a Porcão headband during matches. He received meal vouchers which he gave away to friends, including Kaiser, who sold them on at a sizeable profit.

The players went from Porcão to one of the golden circle of nightclubs: Hippopotamus, Studio C or Caligula. When they closed, usually around five o'clock on Monday morning, Kaiser took them to a secret residence for an after-party. While that was going on, he walked round ensuring none of the guests had a camera.

With no training on Monday, the players would have an after-after-party, usually centred around a barbecue. 'For the players,' says the journalist Martha Esteves, 'Monday was slut day.' Kaiser organised that, too.

His life was not all lad larks. There was that time he went to the police station and took the blame when a Fluminense midfielder knocked somebody out in a nightclub, and even put his hand in his own pocket for the backhander that made it all go away. He also arranged for a girl to have an abortion on behalf of a famous player. 'I've taken the blame so often for others' mistakes,' he says. 'You have no idea. I saved the players' asses. I did things in a way that left no trace. I took better care of others than myself.'

\* \* \*

When you arrive at Estádio General Severiano, the famous old ground of Botafogo, a wall is the first thing that catches the eye. The wall, which stands opposite the stadium, doubles up as a hall-of-fame mural. There are pop-art images of all the club's great players, from Garrincha, Nilton Santos and Didi to modern stars like Clarence Seedorf and Sebastián Abreu. Few clubs celebrate their history like Botafogo, whose place in the pantheon was secured when they provided so many players to the Brazil squads that won the country's first World Cups in 1958 and 1962.

But in 1989, history was all Botafogo had. They were a joke, the man in the bar telling everyone he used to be a contender. They had not won the Brazilian championship or the Campeonato Carioca since 1968, a fact of which opposing fans were sadistically aware. They would slowly count up to twenty-one before chanting 'Happy birthday to you'.

It needed the financial influence of Emil Pinheiro for Botafogo to create a bit of modern history. Sergio Américo, who covered the club for Radio Globo, will never forget the moment the resurgence began with the click of a briefcase catch. It was in 1986, shortly after Pinheiro became involved with the club.

Fernando Macaé, a coveted young midfielder who scored seventeen goals when Bangu almost won the title in 1985, posed in a Flamengo shirt after agreeing a move. He had not yet signed a contract, however, and was persuaded to have a meeting at Pinheiro's house that night. Macaé sat around a table with Américo and Pinheiro, who placed a briefcase on the table and opened it. 'My son,' he said. 'You can have all this up front if you join Botafogo.'

Américo could not take his eyes off the briefcase. 'I have never,' he says, 'seen so much cash in my life.'

Macaé agonised over the decision for the next four seconds before agreeing to join Botafogo. The next day's papers had already gone to press, announcing he was a Flamengo player, when Américo telephoned Radio Globo with the story. The show soon drifted into a two-way phone call between Macaé and the Flamengo president, during which Macaé broke down in tears and apologised. But he still went to Botafogo. It was quite a scoop for Américo – and for Botafogo. It gave Pinheiro the internal clout he needed. After Macaé signed, he effectively ran the club. Though it took a few years to reshape the team, he eventually built a side that could beat anyone. 'Emil was an absurdly wealthy man and built a very capable team,' says Gil. 'A team who couldn't afford rice started eating caviar.'

Botafogo also received a significant helping hand from Castor de Andrade. He owed Pinheiro some money and decided that sacrificing a few footballers made more sense than starting a turf war. Three excellent players – Mauro Galvão, Marinho and Paulinho Criciúma – moved from Bangu to Botafogo.

The club filled a void in his Pinheiro's after the death of his son. The players loved him, and he spent his time at the team hotel telling them stories about fighting in the war. He was also extremely generous when it came to paying anyone, from the tea ladies to Kaiser.

'Emil was very kind,' says the broadcaster José Carlos Araújo. 'He was more of a grandfather figure than a father figure. He wasn't a high-level *bicheiro* like Castor, and he wasn't volatile or short-tempered.'

He had a temperamental moral compass, though, and there were allegations of buying referees and scaring witnesses into silence. But for most, the abiding image of Pinheiro is a cuddly, eccentric little man. 'Dr Emil was really funny,' says Martha Esteves. 'He was tiny and he wore a little wig that would occasionally fall out of place.'

It was not the only thing that fell out of place. Pinheiro was in his sixties, and his physical deterioration meant he was not able to assert his masculinity as he would have liked. This was just before the emergence of Viagra, but

in Brazil there was an alternative – an inflatable prosthetic penis. 'Imagine how much that cost back then!' says
Esteves. 'I said to him, "Dr Emil, you must be over the
moon because I heard you have a new penis." We started
to joke with him, saying he had a permanent stiffy. "Can
you sleep properly?" The daily chat was all about Dr Emil's
penis. You have a guy who was in charge of God knows
how many *bicheiros*, who ran Botafogo, and instead of
interviewing him about football, we'd be talking about his
bionic cock!'

It was the hot topic in the dressing room as well. 'There's
no way you couldn't be aware of it,' says Mauro Galvão. 'I
didn't know how it worked. Sometimes we would get worried because it would sort of poke out.'

\*\*\*

Botafogo had gone ten games without a win, the worst
run anyone could remember, and Emil Pinheiro decided
it was time to front up to the press. Sergio Américo had
been covering the club for fourteen years and felt it was
incumbent upon him to get down to brass tacks.

'Emil Pinheiro, Botafogo haven't won a game for months.
What do you have to say about a crisis at Botafogo?'

Pinheiro drummed his fingers on the table as he considered the question. He leaned backwards in his chair and

looked quizzically under the desk. Then he pulled out the desk drawers and peered inside.

'Sergio Américo, I've looked in the drawer, I've looked in the cupboards, I've looked on the floor and I can't find the Botafogo crisis that you're talking about. You want to know something?'

Pinheiro, a stern expression on his face, maintained steady eye contact with Américo. It was at this precise moment that many of the press had a jolting reminder that, for all Pinheiro's cuddly ways, he was still a *bicheiro*. And *bicheiros* did not take kindly to tough questioning.

Pinheiro stood up slowly and straightened his trousers. 'Sergio Américo!' he barked. As he did so he grabbed his prosthetic penis and squeezed. 'The only Botafogo crisis is here!'

\*\*\*

Kaiser arranged women for Pinheiro for almost five years. 'He had a prosthetic penis and a constant erection. And so he warmed to me. I would say to him, "What do you have that makes all these women want to sleep with you?" Complete lie.'

Emil regularly gave Kaiser the keys to his thirty-five-foot yacht in Angra dos Reis. Their friendship meant Kaiser could stay at Botafogo as long as he liked, even if a couple of players resented the favouritism. Kaiser was not so much teacher's pet as teacher's prodigal. 'Who would dispute me being at the club?' says Kaiser. 'What would they say? His security didn't even let anybody come close to him. The players would gossip about my relationship with Emil. I was his darling. What are you going to do about it?'

There wasn't much Ajaccio could do about it. Kaiser gave them the wrong phone number which meant the only way they could contact him, to check his recovery progress, was by airmail. And airmail had a terrible habit of getting lost in Rio de Janeiro. He did read one letter, written by one of the more straight-laced directors: 'We had very high expectations of you and you have disappointed us at every turn. You might have been great for those people you hung around with off the field but you have served no purpose at this club. When you leave Ajaccio, you will be like a ripped-out page in our history.'

Kaiser put the letter straight in the bin. He was in no hurry to return to Corsica. It was too quiet, too still. 'Ajaccio has nothing,' he says. 'Corsica is a dead island. If you wanted nightlife you had to go to Paris. Ajaccio has bars and cafés. For anybody coming from Rio de Janeiro, Ajaccio has nothing. That's why I stayed in Brazil.'

Even if he wanted to go back to Corsica, this was not the moment. It was the busiest time of year in Brazilian football, and Kaiser had work to do.

# CHAPTER 17

# THE FRIEND OF DIEGO

Kaiser had plenty of parties to organise in 1989, when Botafogo reached the state championship final for the first time in fourteen years. As the victories mounted up, so did the number of superstitions. At a club built on history and mythology, such quirky beliefs were a comfort. Most of them came from Valdir Espinosa, the coach. Martha Esteves, a Flamengo fan who had to cover Botafogo for *Placar* magazine, occasionally asked Espinosa for a cigarette during games. He noticed that, every time she did so, Botafogo won, so for the rest of the season she was forced to chain-smoke within an inch of her arteries. Espinosa also wore the same clothes to every game – black trousers and a white t-shirt. 'I think he had a few pairs,' says Esteves. 'I hope he did.'

Botafogo went unbeaten throughout both stages of the league system, with the winners of each qualifying for the final. A dramatic comeback from 3-1 to 3-3 against Flamengo ultimately meant they qualified for the final against ... Flamengo.

It was an intimidating Flamengo side. Their starting XI included Zico and Renato Gaúcho, as well as four players who would start the World Cup final five years later – Bebeto, Zinho, Aldair and Jorginho – and another, Leonardo, who would have done so had he not been suspended.

The first leg, in the Maracanã, was a 0-0 draw. Botafogo had problems ahead of the second leg: Josimar was enduring a gruesome cocaine comedown, while the forward Maurício, Kaiser's old friend from the club America, had a fever and a grotesque, infected boil on his leg. He could barely walk. Any useful medication would have violated doping tests, so the medical staff ruled him out of the second leg.

Espinosa, who had decided Maurício was another of his lucky charms, ignored medical advice and included him in the team. Maurício spent the first half chasing back after Leonardo. 'I couldn't hack it so at half-time I asked the coach to take me off,' says Maurício. 'He said, "Listen. I'm not taking you off. You're special and you are going to score the winning goal."'

After fifty-seven minutes he did just that, volleying Mazolinha's left-wing cross into the net. The referee missed a sly push on Leonardo, which put him off balance and gave Maurício the space to score.

The goal against Flamengo didn't just change Maurício's life; it has defined it. Three decades later he still dines out on it, and often introduces himself by the name Maurício 89. 'Botafogo was the greatest part of my life story,' he says. 'The goal gave me an amazing professional future. After that I went to play in Spain for Celta Vigo. Then I was called up to play in the World Cup qualifiers and I became Brazilian champion with Sport Club Internacional. Going back to the past gets me emotional and raises my self-esteem. Gosh, it's so exciting. A boy raised in the favela who managed to overcome the obstacles in his life through sport. My mum was a dinner lady and my dad was a taxi driver. I'm a servant and God had a purpose for me with that goal. That day he chose me to bring joy to millions of Botafogo fans.'

And to one in particular. After twenty-one years, Botafogo were champions of Rio again. At the final whistle, as chaotic celebrations went on all around the pitch, Emil Pinheiro gave a television interview that went straight into folklore. 'Now I can die happy,' he said. 'Botafogo are champions.'

Kaiser had been instructed to prepare a country house should Botafogo win or lose. He is keen to stress his role in the team's triumph. 'They were relaxed all season,' he says. 'We saw that on the pitch.'

When Esteves went into the dressing room after the game to interview the players, she was thrown fully clothed into the showers. 'I was trying to interview them but every-body was hugging me and Espinosa said, "You're our rab-bit's foot!" There are still many people who think that I support Botafogo. I have to keep saying, "I don't support Botafogo! I'm Flamengo till I die." There was some magic that year. The stars were aligned for Botafogo.'

The infectious joy of Botafogo's victory made it easier for Esteves to swallow a Flamengo defeat. And at least she could stop chain-smoking those bloody cigarettes.

\*\*\*

Botafogo were not the only ones wanting to end a drought. A month later Brazil hosted the Copa América, a tournament they had not won for forty years. They ended the wait with a stirring victory in which Bebeto emerged as an international star. He was the leading goalscorer with six in the tournament, including a famous flying volley against Argentina.

Everyone at Flamengo had been raving about him for years. 'Bebeto was a teenager when he started to train with us,' says Zico. 'The day before a match we would usually play a practice game. I would always play in defence and from my sixth sense I knew what players would do before they had done it. The first time the ball went to him, I tried to guess what he would do and he turned me. I realised then he was special, that he thought ahead. From that moment I started to nag the management: "We need to look after this kid. Flamengo has found a gem."'

Zico became a mentor to Bebeto. Their relationship was so close that, when Bebeto won the World Cup in 1994, he gave Zico – the greatest Brazilian never to win the World Cup – one of his match shirts. 'It's mounted up in my trophy room,' says Zico. 'It's one of the greatest memories of my career.'

Bebeto played in three World Cups and is fondly remembered for a famous celebration during the 1994 tournament: a few days after the birth of his son, he scored in the quarter-finals against the Netherlands and rocked an imaginary baby with his team-mates.

Although he was slightly overshadowed by Careca, Romário and Ronaldo in the 1990s, he remained a key player even in a 24-carat generation of forwards. Bebeto was also a revelation in Spain with Deportivo de La Coruña, even if his time in Spain is best remembered for something he *didn't* do. On the last day of the 1993–4 season, Deportivo needed to beat Valencia to win the first title in their history. It was 0-0 when they were awarded a penalty in the last minute. The regular taker, Donato, had been substituted, and everyone looked to the star player Bebeto. He bottled it. Instead the responsibility went to the sweeper Miroslav Đjukić, whose tame penalty was easily saved. Romário's Barcelona became champions instead, and it was another six years before Deportivo won their first title. By then, Bebeto was winding down his career with the Japanese club Kashima Antlers.

At the end of the 1989 Copa América, Kaiser was instructed to organise a party for players from Brazil, Argentina and Uruguay. The guest list included the most famous footballer in the world. 'A lot of people ask me, "Do you know Maradona?",' says Kaiser. 'I say, "No, I know Diego Armando". I know the other side of Maradona. The best players are less arrogant than the mediocre ones. I played among a generation of star players. Somebody said to me the other day, "Messi's left foot is the best of all time". If you think that, you've never seen Maradona play. Messi has played for Barcelona with Neymar, Suarez, Iniesta and all the rest. Maradona played on his own. He was left-footed but he used his hands, head, chest and penis.'

Renato Gaúcho, who was back in the Brazil team for the first time since being chucked out of the 1986 World Cup squad, had charged Kaiser with arranging the party. 'Maradona wanted to meet him!' he says. 'Wherever we went, people wanted to talk to Kaiser. Maradona was always extrovert and upbeat. He liked to be around cheerful people – people who were good at talking, especially to women. In other words, Carlos Kaiser.'

After the Copa América final, Kaiser arranged a big night in at a house in Itanhangá in the West Zone. 'I sorted the house and fifty girls,' he says proudly. 'There were a few crazy footballers – Renato, Leandro, Maradona and some Argentines, Hugo de Léon from Uruguay. Trust me, nobody is a bigger party animal than Maradona.' It's not always wise to take Kaiser at his word, but we can probably trust him on that one.

\*\*\*

Brazil were inevitably one of the favourites to win the 1990 World Cup, especially after winning the Copa América. With the tournament taking place in Italy, the coach Sebastião Lazaroni adopted a when-in-Rome approach. He imposed a sweeper system and a European style on a team that was not usually renowned for defensive competence or focus. 'Our defence will have to play a more serious kind of football,' said the striker Careca before the tournament. 'No pussyfooting around. It's not a carnival.'

The symbol of the team was no longer Zico or Socrates but Dunga, a rugged, unsentimental defensive midfielder who personified the change in Brazil's football. They were seen as the antonym to the expressive sides of 1982 and 1986, and many in Brazil regarded the approach as an act of cultural vandalism. The truth was a little more complicated – Brazil still had geniuses to spare in attack – but this was still the most significant change in their football history. 'They went for more athletic players,' says Martha Esteves. 'The transition was way too extreme – they didn't integrate the European strength and power with the Brazilian skill, so we ended up compromising our strengths. The national team was always full of light, technical players, but this was the beginning of the era of the ogre player.'

The ogres still won all three of their group matches, though the scores were not typically Brazilian: 2-1 against Sweden, 1-0 against Costa Rica and Scotland. There was one moment to remember: Careca's beautiful first goal against Sweden, when he went elegantly around the goalkeeper Thomas Ravelli. It was not so much a goal as a free-form dance routine: so smooth and gracefully athletic that you could hear the samba beats as you watched it.

The holders Argentina blundered through their group in third place, which meant they would face Brazil in the last sixteen. To lose at such an early stage of the World Cup was unacceptable for either side; to do so against their most hated rivals was unthinkable.

Brazil dominated the game almost entirely, missing chances and hitting the woodwork three times. Then, with nine minutes to go, all their nightmares came true. Maradona, who had been anonymous all game, produced a legendary assist with a devastating solo run and through ball to Claudio Caniggia, who went around Taffarel to score. Eight years earlier Maradona had been sent off at the World Cup for kicking Brazil's Batista in the balls. Now he did it to the whole country. 'I like Brazilians,' he said, 'but in football I want to beat them to the death.'

It was one of the greatest smash-and-grabs in football history. Not for the first time at the World Cup, Brazil were left bristling with a sense of injustice after being eliminated by Argentina. In 1978, a tournament that Argentina hosted and eventually won, they were drawn with Brazil in the second group stage. The winners would go straight into the final. The scheduling meant that Argentina played their last game after Brazil, so they knew exactly what result they needed. Brazil's 3-1 win over Poland earlier that day meant Argentina needed to beat Peru – who were already out of the tournament – by at least four goals to qualify for the final. They won 6-0, and much was made of the fact that the Peru goalkeeper Ramón Quiroga was born in Argentina. At the time Argentina was controlled by a military junta; it was unthinkable that they should not win the tournament.

Gil, who was part of the Brazil team at that tournament, later worked in Peru as a coach at Alianza Lima. His assistant was César Cueto, the midfielder who had been part of the Peru team against Argentina. One day, Gil arranged a lunch at his house for his coaching staff and told his wife to keep refreshing Cueto's glass. Gil says that, after the umpteenth glass, Cueto said there had been an agreement between the countries.

Argentina's win in 1990 would later be doused in controversy, in what became known as the Holy Water Scandal. During a break in play in the first half, Argentina had given Branco, Brazil's left-back, a water bottle that was allegedly laced with tranquilisers. 'Branco said at half-time that he was feeling really dizzy and kind of stunned,' says Mauro Galvão, who was part of the Brazil team. 'But that could have been for a number of reasons. It's very hard to say anything concrete.'

Carlos Bilardo, the Argentina coach, has never bothered to deny the allegation, and in 2004 Maradona almost exploded with laughter as he discussed the incident on a national TV show, *Mar de Fondo*. 'I could see Branco drink the water and then [the Brazil midfielder] Valdo and others arrived,' he said. 'I was thinking, "Please drink it! Please drink it!".'

Even if the public knew about the Holy Water Scandal at the time, it's unlikely it would have spared the team from being denounced. 'I stopped supporting the national team after that,' says Martha Esteves. 'It wasn't like 1982, when there was a big sadness across the country. In 1990 there was anger at Dunga and Lazaroni. Brazil hates Dunga. He's not a bad person, it's just what he represents as a footballer and a manager.'

Although many of the criticisms were valid, it is rarely acknowledged that they dominated all four of their games, particularly the one against Argentina. 'The criticism was over the top,' says the defender Ricardo Rocha. 'I played in 1990 and 1994, when we won the World Cup, and the best performance in both tournaments was that game against Argentina.'

Nuance was not on the public agenda. It was just about okay for Brazil to fail at a World Cup, and it was just about okay for them to play like a European side – but to do both, while also losing to Argentina, was a guarantee of notoriety.

# CHAPTER 18

# THE MALLRAT

Gonçalves arrived at Rio Sul, his local shopping mall, and saw a commotion in the distance. As a Botafogo player he was used to big crowds, but this was on a different scale. He assumed there was an American pop star in town.

'Hey,' he asked a passer-by, 'what's the fuss over there?'

'Renato Gaúcho's signing some autographs. Have you heard of him? He's a famous footballer.'

Gonçalves had heard of him, though he hadn't heard from him in a while. He knew Renato well from their time together at Flamengo and wandered over to say hello. He was unable to jostle through the shrieking crowd but could just about make out the figure of Renato in his Botafogo kit, cheerfully signing autographs. Gonçalves was about to turn away when he saw Renato move his left hand behind the ear and insouciantly flick his hair forward. Gonçalves recognised that gesture straight away. It was not Renato signing autographs at all.

*** 

For somebody who usually had no money, Kaiser spent a lot of time in shopping malls. It was where footballers went when training finished. Kaiser and his friends have especially fond memories of Rio Sul, the first major shopping tower in the South Zone of Rio. They convened in the same set of seats by the creperie Chez Michou, where they would while away the afternoon and wait to be approached.

'There was a constant flow of women,' says Kaiser. 'They knew the table we would sit at – right by the escalator between the second and third floor. There was never a 0-0 draw at Chez Michou. Back then all the guys were single, just to put the wives at ease. We were approached by actresses and athletes, or wannabe actresses who were looking to jumpstart their careers by cosying up to a footballer and appearing in a photo with them. Life is an exchange.'

If he wasn't with team-mates, Kaiser would walk round chatting people up or inviting them to a VIP section the following weekend. 'In Rio Sul he was the man,' says his friend Gutiérrez. 'He was invincible. He picked up over three hundred women in that place, and they were all hot. His version of the Maracanã was Rio Sul shopping mall.'

Kaiser reinforced his status as a footballer by wearing the training gear of whichever club he was at. He loved designer clothes, but the labels he really craved were Adidas, Umbro, Penalty and Topper – the ones who made the official club kit. If Kaiser looked like a footballer then he felt like a footballer. And if he felt like a footballer then he was one.

'He was so engaging that even he would start to believe his own lie,' says Renato Gaúcho. 'He would plant the idea in people's heads that he was a footballer because he believed within himself that he was a footballer. He even was a footballer, doing the same things a footballer would, up to a certain point.'

Sometimes he would go into the men's room and dunk his mullet to make it look like it was drenched in sweat from training. He also drew attention to himself by talking loudly in French. On one occasion Luiz Maerovitch, an old friend of Kaiser's who is president of the Jewish social centre Hebraica, bumped into him one evening at Rio Sul. Kaiser was wearing a full first-team kit, as if he had just come from a match. His socks were rolled up to the knee. And he had sunglasses on.

'Luiz, what brings you here?'

'I'm getting a birthday present for my mother-in-law. How about you?'

'I'm promoting myself.'

Maerovitch looked Kaiser up and down.

'Man, you look ridiculous.'

'I know.'

'What?'

'I said, I know.'

'So why are you doing it?'

'I told you, I'm promoting myself. You see all those people looking over at us? They're not looking at your bald dome, Luiz. They're looking at me, because they think I'm a footballer.'

\*\*\*

Kaiser always wanted to be at the same club as Renato Gaúcho. The Italian giants AS Roma had a full quota of foreign players, alas, so he had to wait until Renato returned to Flamengo. He did not train but was able to hang around as Renato's friend and errand boy, which in turn enabled him to get the usual collection of Kaiserbilia: official kit, photos with star players. If he thought it would help, Kaiser would steal a Flamengo serviette.

Throughout 1989, Kaiser divided his time between Flamengo, Botafogo and Fluminense. It was not just in sexual relationships that Kaiser rejected monogamy. The more teams he was associated with, the more his great scam was able to perpetuate itself. His attachment to Flamengo grew when the club signed the powerful striker Luís Carlos Tóffoli in 1990. He was also born in Rio Grande do Sul, like Renato and Kaiser, and was best known by the nickname Gaúcho. He became great friends with Kaiser and Renato Gaúcho, and though Kaiser had an ever-increasing social circle, he was most likely to be seen demonstrating a ferocious lust for life along with the two Gaúchos. There is one picture of the three, taken at a party at a Brahma brewery. They are all wearing Brahma vests and identimullets, while Renato has a pink cap that reads PAKALOLO, a word for a particularly potent form of marijuana. Kaiser is looking lasciviously at the camera while the others are a picture of studied indifference. For the next decade, they were inseparable.

\*\*\*

Kaiser was in Rio Sul with a group of players one afternoon when they noticed a crowd gathering in the distance.

'What's going on over there?' said Kaiser.

'Maybe Renato Gaúcho's signing autographs,' sniggered Gonçalves.

They soon realised what the fuss was about: a *Playboy* cover girl had arrived, and the mall had come to a standstill.

'Kaiser, I'll bet you ten thousand cruzeiros you can't get her number,' said Gutiérrez.

'Don't insult me,' sniffed Kaiser. 'You can't put a price on true love.'

He walked over and started chatting. Five minutes later he returned with a number.

'Kaiser, how the fuck did you do that?'

'A magician never reveals his secrets.'

'Come on, what did you say to her?'

'I told her to watch the football on Sunday because I was going to dedicate my next goal to her live on Globo. That broke the ice, and it was easy after that. Just like Romário only needs two seconds to score in the box, I only need two seconds to score with a girl.'

\*\*\*

The malls were not just daytime hangouts; most of them had nightclubs on the top floor. Kaiser was the PR manager of Maxim's, the Rio Sul club that was co-owned by the agent Frankie Henouda and the celebrated fashion designer Pierre Cardin. It had its own heliport and was a favourite haunt of visiting superstars, particularly during festivals like Rock in Rio.

The list of those schmoozed by Kaiser includes Mick Jagger, Lionel Ritchie, Freddie Mercury, Guns N' Roses and the Jackson 5. 'They wanted to meet the big fish,' says Kaiser. 'And who was with the big fish? Me.'

As well as being teetotal, Kaiser has never touched cigarettes or drugs in his life. Instead he got high on status, especially when international superstars were involved. 'He wanted fame to show that he was doing well, and power to show that he was the man,' says Luiz Maerovitch. 'He was a brilliant promoter. He had a lot of very good job offers in that area that he never pursued. He wasn't interested.'

If the bouncers did not recognise a star – as happened with George Benson and Freddie Mercury – Kaiser was the man who sorted things out. 'I took Freddie Mercury straight to the VIP section,' says Kaiser, shaking his head. 'That guy did too many drugs.'

Kaiser could use a broom to sweep up all the names he drops, yet these are stories nobody ever questions.

'If he said, "I went to the Oscars' after-party at Robert De Niro's house", I wouldn't doubt him,' says Alexandre Torres. 'That could actually have happened because he could have charmed his way in. But any story he tells about being on the pitch is a lie.'

\*\*\*

Top: 'Rundown houses, violence everywhere': Mena Barreto Street in Rio de Janeiro, where Kaiser grew up.

The two sides to Kaiser's nickname: the imperious West Germany sweeper Franz Beckenbauer and the chubby beer bottle.

Right and bottom: Kaiser's first feature photoshoot, in the colours of his French club Gazélec Ajaccio.

Renato Gaúcho, Kaiser's best friend, was the Brazilian superstar Europe never knew. When he won the Campeonato Carioca with Fluminense in 1995, he dressed up as the King of Rio the next morning.

Below: Renato poses with Kaiser at his annual New Year party in Buzios; the two are joined by the former Flamengo striker Gaúcho at a Brahma beer party.

The Independiente squad that beat Liverpool to become world champions in 1984.

Kaiser hated alcohol but had enough moral flexibility
to promote beer if there was something in it for him.

Kaiser shows off his luscious mullet, and some dubious 1980s fashion.

**34 – ESPORTES** — O DIA — Rio de Janeiro, domingo, 13 de outubro de 1995

# Unidos: o time dos desempregados

EMYGDIO FELIZARDO FILHO

Até 'estrangeiros' na fila de espera

---

*Jornal da Zona Sul* — 15

## Craque troca chuteira por sunga e microfone

### RECADO DO CORAÇÃO

*Kayser, infeliz no amor e no futebol*

### Ex-craque da seleção é vítima de racismo

---

**CLUB DE REGATAS VASCO DA GAMA**
DEPARTAMENTO MÉDICO
RECEITA

Carlos Henrique Lopes

08/06/91

---

Seja você o repórter da sua rua – Ligue-nos e informe

**BRECHÓ ANARKIA**
USADOS / NOVOS
MIL DETALHES

**QUEROMAIS**

**J. B. FOT E PRODUÇ**
BENTO USE
CATETE - T

---

**Gazelec Football Club Ajaccien**
G.F.C.
Ajaccio

**CARTE JOUEUR**
Saison 19 89 / 19 90
Nom. HENRIQUE RAPOSO
Prénom. CARLOS
Catégorie: SÉNIOR
le Président — le Titulaire — Carte strictement personnelle.

**Ajaccien**
SAISON 19 / 1994
Nom. HENRIQUE RAPOSO
Prénom. CARLOS
catégorie: PROFESSIONEL
Carte strictement personnelle.

---

# Müller retorna ao time e com ele as esperanças do América

*Müller e Renato, esperanças de recuperação no América*

Kaiser had a range of self-publicity tools:
newspaper articles, ID cards, even official prescriptions.

Top: Castor de Andrade, the most dangerous man in Rio, was a father figure to Kaiser at AC Bangu. Castor (meaning 'beaver' in Portuguese) had such success at Bangu that a beaver was added to their kit in tribute.

Left: Brazil's 1986 squad, minus the exiled Renato Gaúcho, reached the quarter-final in Mexico.

Bottom: The unknown full-back Josimar became an overnight star, but the romantic perfectionist Tele Santana again fell short of winning the World Cup.

Right: Looking the part: Kaiser loved designer clothes, but the labels he really craved were Adidas, Umbro, Topper and Pony – the ones who made the official kit.

Kaiser was friends with the greats of Brazilian football, including Renato Gaúcho, Mauricio (below) and Carlos Alberto Torres (bottom right). And if he wasn't friends, he would manufacture a photo opportunity – as he did with Zico (right) before the 1986 World Cup.

Top: The Rio Sul shopping mall, where Kaiser chatted up women, signed autographs pretending to be someone else and generally promoted himself.

Middle: Kaiser with Marcella Mendes, the love of his life.

Bottom: Kaiser in 2018, doing what he does best: holding court and telling stories.

When Kaiser wasn't at the mall, he was usually at the beach, every self-respecting Carioca's second home. Kaiser hung out with friends, strutted round in dangerously snug Speedos, chatted up strangers and diligently promoted himself. 'The beach was always my favourite place,' he says. 'You get there and from the moment you hit the sand, you and the women either look good or not. There's no way of hiding it. And I had nothing to hide anyway.'

And Kaiser did look bloody good. He was bronzed, with prominent cheekbones, the ever-present Speedos and, most of the time, a taut physique. His facial expression alternated between a warm, conspiratorial smile and an impassive, knowing look that hinted at an ocean of lust below the surface.

Most of Rio's finest footballers spent their days off at the beach – and sometimes their days on, whether before training, after training or occasionally when they were sup-posed to be at training. 'When you have a day off in other cities around Brazil, there's nothing to do,' says Renato Gaúcho. 'In Rio you go to the beach. You can sit next to a millionaire or be next to a guy who doesn't even have enough money to eat. And every kind of person is making the most of a sunny day and the sea, having a beer, looking at pretty women and a great view.'

Kaiser was rarely happier than when he spent a year looking after a seaside apartment in Leme that belonged to Henouda. He would train – at least, he would *go* to training – then have lunch at Marius's Steakhouse before heading across the road to watch a kickabout or a game of footvolley. 'A twenty-four-hour day goes by and you spend twelve of those on the beach,' he says. 'I had a whale of a time. Ten months on my own with a beach view in the paradise that is Leme. It was a joke.'

It wasn't so funny when Kaiser chatted up the wrong woman on the beach one afternoon. She already had a husband, who was swimming when Kaiser tried it on. The husband was also a member of the militia and he didn't care who Kaiser's friends were. Attempting to cuckold a militiaman was not Kaiser's smartest move; for the next few months he kept a very low profile.

It was on the beach, usually while watching a game of footvolley, that Kaiser first met many of the greats in his social circle, from Renato Gaúcho to Ricardo Rocha. He went to kickabouts all over Rio, both on the sand and the grass: Monday night in Barra, Montenegro beach in Ipanema with the Fluminense players, Saturday morning in Recreio in Barra da Tijuca with Maerovitch and the Jewish community.

It was there, Maerovitch says, that Kaiser was actually christened – not when he was a kid whom people compared to Franz Beckenbauer. There was a popular beer called Kaiser, which came in short, fat bottles. Kaiser, who was chubby at the time, was given the nickname by one of the players. It stuck.

The kickabouts Kaiser went to may have been informal, but he was still loath to get involved unless it served a broader purpose. No game was ready to start until Kaiser had hobbled onto the scene to tell everyone about another frustrating injury that was going to keep him out of action. 'Whenever he turned up at the beach I made a point of throwing him the ball,' says the actor Eri Johnson. 'He would always catch it. He never controlled it with his feet. I realised he was good with coconuts, not with balls. That's our star player, Kaiser the faker.'

Johnson saw plenty of examples of Kaiser's ability to avoid playing football. On one occasion, Kaiser brokered a deal for three celebrities to play in a match at Club Med – Johnson, the striker Gaúcho and Kaiser. He deliberately left his boots behind, then complained they had been lost in transit by the chauffeur Club Med had sent to pick him up. When it was suggested that Kaiser might consider giving back his appearance fee, he asked how many other star footballers would give up a whole day without being paid, and pointed out that it was hardly his fault if the idiot chauffeur had lost his kitbag. Not only did he keep the money, he was given extra to buy a replacement pair of boots.

\*\*\*

When Kaiser did deign to play football, it was invariably to impress watching women. Kaiser knew they would only be half paying attention, and that some didn't like football anyway, so if he avoided the ball nobody would realise that he was a fish on dry land. It became a game of cat and mouse. Players would try to pass to Kaiser, who would make a subtly different run and then bemoan the poor pass into him. 'It was so funny,' says Júnior Negão. 'It's like somebody who's scared of blood wanting to be a doctor.' Marcelo Campello thinks the reason Kaiser played as a centre-forward is because it's easier to hide from the game. The rhythm of football is such that, in most games, the striker has the fewest touches.

To the untrained eye, Kaiser's inability would not have been obvious, certainly not on the days when he success-fully avoided the ball or was able to play low-risk passes to others. 'If the ball did come to him he would do a little feint and get rid of it straight away,' says Gustavo, who has known Kaiser since they were at school together planning bomb scares. 'He would always act like a player-manager on the pitch, thumping his chest and bossing everybody around in a loud voice to impress the women.'

One player was so irritated by Kaiser's fraudulent strut that he nailed him with a vicious two-footed tackle. This time Kaiser's screams of pain were real; he still has a scar on his ankle.

Kaiser loved the reflected glamour from being among the superstars of Brazilian football, and the networking opportunities it provided. That was particularly true when Júnior, the Flamengo legend, had his end-of-season beach kickabout. This was one time when Kaiser desperately wanted to be on the pitch. 'He was always trying to meddle in the professional stuff because he saw himself as a professional,' says Júnior. 'But although the end-of-season friendlies were a bit of fun, everybody wanted to win. There was no room for Kaiser in a team that wanted to win.'

Those games were a football festival in more ways than one – the match was accompanied by bars, a barbecue and usually hundreds of supporters. In those days, musicians, actors and footballers mixed all the time. Then again, football was part of the arts in Brazil. Legendary singers like Jorge Ben and João Nogueira would even go on the Flamengo bus to matches on the Maracanã.

'It was amazing,' says the singer and Flamengo fan Bebeto. 'Life was simple and everybody was happy. At the end of the season there would be beach football and a party on Copacabana. Players came from São Paulo to join in the fun. We would all play against each other. Musicians and footballers still mix but it was simpler before, more natural, more casual. It was very easy to go up to people. It's difficult nowadays. You don't have those gatherings like you did back in the 1980s. At the end, a group of people would go out for dinner at Porção and another group would stay on the beach drinking beer until the sun came up again.'

When Kaiser did join in, it rarely went well. Júnior Negão recalls a regular over-thirty-fives friendly in Leme involving Romário and other Brazilian greats. One day they were a player short and persuaded Kaiser to get involved. 'I'd never seen the guy play but I thought he must know how to move the ball and shoot as every Brazilian does,' he says. 'After five minutes everybody started complaining to me: "Kaiser's too crap, it won't work". We had to play with a man short. That's when I realised how charming he must have been to get a contract. Every Brazilian can control the ball and shoot – it's not hard – but Kaiser really couldn't do that.'

A similar thing happened during a pre-season kick-about, when, after Kaiser endured a challenging first half, a player called Pedrinho spent the entire half-time break abusing him. 'Get lost,' he shouted. 'You can't play with us. We're going to play with ten men instead because you're so crap. You don't even kick the ball. You just want to run up and down the pitch!'

All the players laughed uproariously at Kaiser, who seethed internally. When the second half started, Kaiser began chatting to the groups of people watching the game.

He wanted to find out a bit more about Pedrinho. Kaiser soon learned that Pedrinho had a thing for a young girl called Nathalia, who was watching the game, and started to chat her up himself. Pedrinho, who was still playing, watched the situation unfold and raged with impotent fury. He even tried to leave the game before being pressured into staying.

'We're already down to fucking ten men because of you,' said one player. 'You're not leaving us with nine players.'

With a couple of minutes to go, and Pedrinho at boiling point, Kaiser and Nathalia walked off hand in hand.

'He was always like that,' says Kaiser's friend Alexandre Couto. 'If somebody took the piss out of him in a nasty way, he got his own back.'

Although Kaiser tried to hang around most kickabouts, he knew that a few were off-limits – particularly those that were organised by the legendary Romário. There were times when the two got on well, especially when Romário needed Kaiser to arrange something for him, but there was a line that Kaiser was not allowed to cross – the one that separated the real footballers from the fantasists. 'Romário used to go to Barra da Tijuca, not Ipanema. And Kaiser was the Ipanema phenomenon,' says Eri Johnson. 'If he'd been over here in Barra, Romário would have said to him, "Hey, mate, let me tell you something. You're crap. You can't even do a kick up. You haven't scored or done anything, so I'm going to tell you something: Scram! Get lost! Cheers for coming!"

\*\*\*

Luiz Maerovitch picked Kaiser up every Saturday morning on his way to the kickabout in Barra da Tijuca. On this occasion, Kaiser emerged from his flat with a friend called Eva who, he said, wanted to see him in action. Maerovitch wondered what Kaiser was up to. Surely the last thing he wanted her to do was see him play football?

When they arrived at the venue, Kaiser announced he and Eva would chat in the car for a few minutes and then he would join the game. At half-time there was still no sign of Kaiser. When the players looked over, the windows of the car were steamed up and it was gently rocking in a manner that suggested Kaiser and Eva had not been passing the time discussing the prose style of Nelson Rodrigues.

Five minutes before the end of the second half, with the match level at 2-2, a dishevelled Kaiser emerged from the car and announced he wanted to come on. Kaiser's first touch of the ball was his last. A shot hit the post and fell to him in front of an open goal. He swept it in, whipped off his shirt in celebration and announced his departure.

'I can't play with amateurs! You're such amateurs. I can't play with you.'

Kaiser ran straight off the field and back into the car. It was soon rocking back and forth again.

\*\*\*

In June 1990, Kaiser decided it was probably time to show his face in Ajaccio. He apologised for the breakdown in communication and arranged to return – provided they paid his airfare – to discuss his contract, which was due to expire at the end of the month. Kaiser timed his return for the end of the season, just when all the players were going on their summer holidays. Most of the directors wanted rid of Kaiser, but those who had been to his parties were keen for him to stay. Eventually Kaiser was given a new four-year contract with a low basic wage and a pay-as-you-play bonus structure. Kaiser knew there was no chance of him earning any bonuses; but he also knew his basic wage was money for nothing. Kaiser spent a few weeks in Corsica, mostly organising parties, before one of the directors approached him one day with sad news: his grandmother had died. The news, he said, had been relayed to the club by Kaiser's cousin in Rio de Janeiro. In reality, Kaiser had placed the call himself, scratching the mouthpiece of the phone as he spoke to simulate a dodgy overseas line.

Kaiser returned to Rio. Ajaccio's Brazilian colony was dwindling – Alexandre Couto and Renato Mendes Mota had already returned, and, when Fabinho moved from Corsica to Saudi Arabia in 1991, Kaiser had even less incentive to return.

By then, Kaiser had already had another overseas adventure. In January 1991, he had a spell with the Texas club El Paso. 'You can never be 100 per cent sure with Kaiser but I think that happened,' says Fabinho. 'I was in Rio on my winter break. I took him to the airport and saw him go through check-in for a flight to El Paso.'

El Paso were coached by Kaiser's friend Marinho Chagas, a blond left-back who represented Brazil at the 1974 World Cup and later played for New York Cosmos alongside Pelé, Carlos Alberto Torres and the real Kaiser, Franz Beckenbauer. Although Kaiser was officially affiliated to Ajaccio, and unofficially to Botafogo, he signed a three-month contract.

Kaiser spent most of his time by the hotel pool nursing a fictitious injury. He also went to Las Vegas with a senior director. 'I could tell straight away he was gay,' says Kaiser. 'He was still in the closet so I sorted out some men for him. I didn't blackmail him. I didn't need to.'

After a few weeks, a homesick Kaiser complained to Marinho Chagas that he wanted to return to a proper club in Rio.

'This club is really amateur. I can't stay here, it's not going to work for me. I'm too professional.'

'What about the money?' said Marinho Chagas.

'They can fuck themselves with the money!'

They couldn't actually do that, literally or metaphorically: Kaiser pocketed the signing-on fee and went back to Brazil.

# CHAPTER 19

# THE LADYKILLER

His name is Kaiser and he is an addict. 'I played football because it gave me easier access to women,' he says. 'Everything I did was connected to sex. I have no other hobbies. My whole life has revolved around sex. I have a disease, like they say Michael Douglas has. If you put a hot girl in the stands and tell me, "She's going to shag you", I'll score a hat-trick right now.'

In his heyday, Kaiser had sex everywhere, from nightclub toilets to church chapels, the latter during a friend's wedding. At times he is introspective and apologetic; at others he takes unashamed pride as he dispenses sermons from the lad bible. Occasionally he manages both at the same time.

He bragged that he was incapable of love; that no woman could penetrate his heart. But it was clear he would do anything for lust. 'I swear on my eyesight and my health, easily over a thousand women,' he says, like a matador talking about his conquests in El Ruendo. 'If sex was football, I'd be Pelé. If women were money, I'd be a millionaire.'

Kaiser would chat people up anywhere, from nightclub dance floors to bus stops. 'If there were girls at a funeral or in a bakery,' he says, 'I'd go there.' He changed his approach depending on the circumstances and told women what they wanted to hear. It might be that they were talking to a famous footballer; that he could get them a modelling contract or an acting audition; that he was a complex, sensitive soul. Whatever it took. 'I wasn't as famous as some of the players,' he says. 'So I had to use the brains God gave me. I don't see myself as good-looking, but most footballers are ugly so someone like me becomes a stud. Especially as I knew how to say the right things at the right time. If you let me open my mouth, I was in.'

Kaiser's restlessness and preference for short-term relationships, whether with women or football clubs, meant he didn't mind if the lie eventually unravelled. All that mattered was the moment. Nor did he care about leagues of attraction. He had the chutzpah to chat up any woman in Rio. A number of players use the same phrase to describe Kaiser: *cara de pau*, which literally means 'wood face' but translates as a mixture of cheekiness and shamelessness. 'That girl everybody is too scared to go up to, he approaches,' says Gustavo. 'He's got nothing to lose.'

The group would place bets over whether Kaiser could woo a woman of their choice, or slap down a load of money as an incentive for him to do so. One day, while they were enjoying a post-kickabout beer on Copacabana, Kaiser was encouraged to approach Isadora Ribeiro, a famous actress who was notorious for giving the shortest shrift to male admirers. The stakes were raised accordingly.

'Kaiser, this one is beyond even you. Never mind money, if you get her number I'll buy you a fucking apartment in Barra.'

'Just like Romário only needs two seconds to score in the box, I only need two seconds to score with a girl.'

Kaiser accepted the challenge and wandered off, stopping to talk to a small boy. The players were in hysterics. Kaiser had bottled it, or at the very least was buying himself time while he tried to think of a scam. A few minutes later, when Ribeiro went into the water, Kaiser followed her. Then, out of nowhere, he started splashing frantically and diving under the water.

'My watch!' shouted Kaiser. 'My Rolex! That cost $50,000!'

'What the hell?' said Ribeiro. 'Really? You've lost your watch?'

She started to help Kaiser look for his watch for a few minutes, at which point Kaiser called off the search, announcing that there were more important things in life than status symbols. As the two of them emerged from the water, a nervous child came up to Kaiser and asked for his autograph – the same boy Kaiser had spoken to (and paid) a couple of minutes earlier. Ribeiro questioned why Kaiser was being asked for his autograph, at which point Kaiser put himself in shy, modest mode, eventually allowing the fact that he was a famous footballer to be coaxed out of him.

Kaiser walked past his friends with Ribeiro, haughtily ignoring their laddish cheers. He sat down and spent the rest of the afternoon chatting with her. 'He ended up leaving the beach with her,' says Alexandre Couto. 'As he was leaving everybody started applauding. He says after that he went out with her. Whether that's true I don't know but the first part is – I saw it all. He was such an alpha male. When people doubted him, he always proved them wrong.'

He pulled a similar trick at the beach when he had announced to anyone who would listen that his BMW had been stolen. And apparently random approaches from fans were commonplace. On one occasion he told his dentist friend Ricardo Ostenhas to ask for an autograph when he was with a woman, and then administered a theatrical bollocking to him for intruding upon his private time. 'Can't you see I'm with this beautiful girl?'

Kaiser believed in what teachers called guided discovery. 'You don't need to go around with a sign saying, "I'm a footballer",' he says. 'I would set up scenarios so they would find out, like not having to pay the bill at a restaurant.'

The most extravagant example of that occurred in January 1989. When Kaiser heard Ajaccio wanted to sign his friend Renato Mendes Mota, he took the opportunity to impress a girl he liked. Kaiser arranged to meet her for lunch by the pool at the Copacabana Palace, where they bumped into Mendes Mota and some agents who were negotiating the transfer. Mota was represented by an Italian called Antonio Rossellini, who had been briefed as to his role in Kaiser's story. The agents representing Ajaccio were introduced to Carlos Henrique Raposo rather than Carlos Kaiser, and therefore had no idea they were actually talking to the black sheep of the club.

They were happy to help out Mota and Raposo, especially as it was in return for a sizeable favour. They wanted to buy some classic football shirts while in Brazil, and Mendes Mota recommended his friend, Mr Raposo, as somebody who could help. He sold them a Botafogo shirt, worn by the great Jairzinho in 1968, for a bargain R$500. It literally reeked of authenticity. No wonder: Kaiser had worn it while running on the beach. It was a modern replica of the classic Botafogo kit that he washed repeatedly until it started to fade and shrink.

After the terms of Mota's transfer were provisionally agreed, talk turned to Raposo. And so, for the next hour, representatives of Ajaccio made an extravagant song and dance about wanting to sign a player they already owned, purely so he could impress a girl and make her think he was on the brink of a bumper payday.

'Look, if we sign Renato we'll already be at our limit of four foreign players – Renato, Fabio Barros, Alexandre Couto and Carlos Kaiser. Once we can get rid of Kaiser we can sign you. He's gone AWOL.'

'This delay is not good for me,' said Kaiser. 'What are the fans going to think? They have already read about me in the local newspaper.'

'You think we don't know that? I got to work last week and there was graffiti on the door of the club office saying "WE WANT CARLOS HENRIQUE RAPOSO".'

'Look, graffiti doesn't pay my bills. When are we going to sort this?'

At this point Rossellini, playing the role of Kaiser's agent, interjected. 'You have two more weeks. We can't wait any longer.'

'I want to come to Corsica,' said Kaiser. 'But I need to sort my future out, and I need financial security. I've had offers from Palmeiras and also from Roma and Brescia in Italy.'

The Ajaccio representatives promised they would sign Raposo the moment they got rid of Kaiser.

\*\*\*

Long before football's data revolution, Kaiser was crunching the numbers. Before a night out, or an afternoon at the mall, he would write his number on thirty or forty pieces of paper and hand them out as flyers. He didn't care about the rejections: even five out of thirty was better than nought out of nought.

'He was always with beautiful women,' said Carlos Alberto Torres. 'He was quite handsome. He was no stud but he was decent looking and he would always be hanging out with really pretty women in Rio.' Kaiser dated Dora Bria, the famous windsurfer, for a few months before she found out his story was built of sand. 'I've slept with many famous people,' he says. 'The girls on the "Superfantastico" show. Singers. Famous foreign tennis players. French actresses. I don't want to incriminate anybody. A lot of them are married. Many of them have kids now.'

Some of them had grandkids then. Kaiser's list of conquests includes a few who paid for the experience, some believing they were sleeping with Renato Gaúcho. 'I've slept with women for money,' he says. 'Older women, when I was twenty and they were forty-five, fifty, sixty. I've slept with a seventy-year-old! With no Viagra!'

It often seemed like Kaiser's life was one big porn film, so you can probably guess what happened next. His cousin Paulo Tomé was invited to audition for some adult entertainment, and Kaiser volunteered to offer moral support.

What happened next doesn't need to be described in forensic detail. But after extensive negotiations, Kaiser ended up as part of a scene that was not in the original script. He received the approval of the leading lady, who recommended him to the executive producer. 'You could put him in a scene with two hundred people around him and he won't flake,' she said. 'The guy is proper talented.'

Sadly for the adult entertainment cognoscenti, the film was never made.

\*\*\*

Kaiser had a phone book with over a thousand women's numbers. He wrote each and every one backwards, just in case it was ever stolen. That book was his most important possession, not least because it made him almost indispensable. 'He became known among the players here in Rio,' says Gonçalves. 'We'd say, "Let's go out to Studio C tonight. Call Kaiser. Get him to bring along some girls."'

Kaiser, you suspect, has enough dirt to fill newspapers for months. 'If he becomes as famous as he thinks he was in the past, loads of people are in trouble,' laughs Renato Gaúcho. 'And I'm not the only one implicated in the stories, I'm telling you.' Kaiser's loyalty is too great for him to name the protagonist in certain stories: like the clean-cut footballer who hid in the boot of a car when Kaiser drove him to an orgy, or the star whose gold cocaine box was put in Kaiser's safe-keeping at parties.

As Kaiser says, life is an exchange. He might arrange female companionship for a doctor, who would then sign him off indefinitely from playing football because of a muscle problem that stemmed from a hitherto undiagnosed peanut allergy. He also arranged women for older former players and especially the older *bicheiros*. Everyone was in his debt. And he knew that everyone liked women. 'I found out what you needed and I would exploit that need. Your weak point. What you like.'

Kaiser also played Cupid for his less famous friends. 'He would approach on our behalf with that Casanova style,' says Luiz Maerovitch. 'There's a saying here: "If you don't have money you tell stories." So he would tell stories very well.'

One night, Kaiser and Maerovitch went over to two women in a nightclub. Maerovitch smiled nervously, unable to hear what Kaiser was saying to them. A couple of minutes later, he was surprised to find out that he was the owner of Pirelli, one of the world's biggest tyre-manufacturing companies. 'The woman was impressed before I'd said a word to her,' he says. 'Kaiser pulled almost every single girl he chatted up – whether it was for himself or someone else. He was one of the only guys in Rio de Janeiro with such reputation and with such charm.'

Vinicius Diek, who runs a kiosk near the beach in Leme, wondered why he was suddenly surrounded by women on a night out. Kaiser explained that he was a world-famous UFC star.

Gutiérrez, another of Kaiser's friends, resembled the Flamengo player Ailton, with inevitable consequences. 'The girls would ask me for a Flamengo shirt or tickets to the Maracanã,' he says. 'I would have to buy them myself. I spent loads of money on that, but it was great value because the girls were super-hot. Whenever we went after a couple of girls Kaiser would always tell me to keep my mouth shut. When I came along he'd done all the ground-work. I just had to score the penalty.'

Kaiser set 'Ailton' up with at least twenty people. He got a nasty surprise when he went for an MRI scan and found the secretary was somebody he had recently spent the night with. As he scribbled his real name on the rele-vant form, he nervously explained that Ailton was just a footballer nickname. There was a happier ending when Gutiérrez met his wife Celeste through his alter ego. 'I really have to thank Kaiser for that introduction. I've been in a relationship with a wonderful person for twenty-five years. He was the one who introduced me. I met her on the beach when he was flirting with her sister ...'

# CHAPTER 20

# THE BLACK MAGIC PATIENT

Most people say Kaiser couldn't play football if his sex life depended on it. That was certainly the opinion of the Vasco da Gama players when he returned to the club in 1991 and was dragged into a game of piggy in the middle. It was Bebeto, the star striker who had moved from Flamengo, who suggested that Vasco allow Kaiser to do a bit of training while he regained fitness.

'He was dashing from one end to the other,' laughs Bebeto. 'He was sweating loads! I thought he was going to have a heart attack. The ball went this way and that way but everybody said, "Get him out, get him out. Otherwise he's going to die. You're going to kill Kaiser." All of the players agreed: "Kaiser is so crap!".'

Kaiser pulled up nursing his thigh and his pride.

'You're fine, aren't you?' said Bebeto quietly.

'Yep. I just can't handle it.'

The players liked having Kaiser around so much that they tolerated his technical imperfections, and even defended him – 'He's coming back from injury, cut him some slack' – if a member of the coaching staff criticised him. 'I held the group together,' says Kaiser. 'I was probably more useful off the field than on it.'

Probably.

\*\*\*

While Kaiser agrees he was at his most useful off the field, he doesn't accept he was useless on it. 'I had talent, but I didn't like football,' he sniffs. 'When people say, "Kaiser wasn't a good player" … they're missing the point. The reason Kaiser wasn't a good player is because they're comparing him to the players he hung around with: Ricardo Rocha, Romário, Bebeto, Renato Gaúcho. In today's generation I'd be a star player. Nobody plays in the teams I played at without being good. Why do you think my nickname is Kaiser? Why do you think the Fluminense players called me Maradona?'

\*\*\*

Kaiser arrived at the Vasco training crowd in a cheery mood, looking forward to another day of doing absolutely nothing. He wasn't whistling such a happy tune when Paulo Angioni, Vasco's director of football, came over to say hello. Angioni told Kaiser that the club were so desperate to see him play that they had instructed a black magic priest called Pai Santana to cure him.

'Oh my God, that was such a funny day,' says Bebeto. 'The black magic priest had all his spells. He was saying, "Come here, my son, come here." Kaiser got really scared.'

Kaiser didn't believe in voodoo. He believed in voo-don't. As the priest prepared to go to work, Kaiser gave him some advice. 'Take your money, man. There's nothing wrong with me. There are some things black magic can't cure. Take your money and don't bother doing your thing because I intend to stay injured for the rest of my life.'

Kaiser also bribed Carlão and Gato, the Vasco masseuse and kit man respectively, to corroborate his injury stories and give him all kinds of elaborate treatments. Whenever the management team asked if Kaiser was ready to train, Carlão said he needed a few more weeks' recovery.

During that time Kaiser became friendly with an emerging attacker called Edmundo, who went on to become one of the best players in Brazil. His encyclopaedic knowledge of football helped him pinpoint the most exciting young players in Brazil, primarily so that he could befriend them before they started to climb to the top of the ladder.

Bebeto has one other memory of Kaiser's time at Vasco da Gama – that he was constantly negotiating a transfer to Europe on one of the landlines at the club. 'He'd speak in Portuguese,' says Bebeto. 'I was thinking, "How does that work? Are you going to France speaking Portuguese?" I took the phone from him and there was nobody on the other end. He was talking to himself.'

On another occasion, Kaiser was caught having a heated argument about unpaid wages – with the speaking clock.

# CHAPTER 21

# THE FREELOADER

Kaiser made up for having no money by being extremely economical with the truth. His ability to freeload was legendary. 'He was always hanging out at the best spots, and he was always broke,' says Renato Gaúcho, smiling and shaking his head. 'How do you manage that?'

He did it by creating a cornucopia of exchanges, many of which ran simultaneously, to ensure his needs were met. They ranged from the shameless to the subtle, the explicit to the unspoken.

He might promise to bring Carlos Alberto Torres or another superstar to a restaurant – thus giving it an instant hit of prestige – in return for a month of free meals. Journalists would write articles about him in return for a prime reservation at Porcão, the famous steakhouse, or entry to the VIP section of Hippopotamus.

Sometimes the exchanges were particularly intricate. Kaiser would promise a journalist an exclusive interview with a star player if they wrote a profile about his career. He would use that profile to help secure a VIP section at a nightclub, and then invite beautiful women to come to the party, promising them footballers at every table. The promise of the women ensured the players came along. If one of them met somebody he liked, he would thank Kaiser by giving that exclusive interview.

And the whole thing kept on perpetuating itself.

It was quite a juggling act. Journalists, players, managers, directors, women, restaurateurs, nightclub owners: Kaiser had to make sure his story was consistent with all of them. 'I'd need a completely annotated chronogram in order to not trip over my own lies,' says Roger Flores, the former Brazil international who became friends with Kaiser in the 1990s. 'I'd never manage to live a lie for so long. Look, there are people like Kaiser in Rio, who tell stories on a night out: "I'm on holiday in Brazil. I play in China. I play in Indonesia." But they do it once or twice. Kaiser did it every day for decades.'

He managed not only to do that but also to create a web of lies so elaborate that nobody could remember who vouched for him in the first place. 'His greatest quality,' says Ricardo Rocha, 'is that he's friends with your friend.'

Edgar Pereira compares Kaiser to one of the world's most famous con men: Frank Abagnale, who was played in the Steven Spielberg film *Catch Me If You Can* by Leonardo DiCaprio. 'There's a scene where DiCaprio is about to be caught and he hides himself in a big group of women. Every time I see that I think of Kaiser.' When he is asked whether there were any pretenders to Kaiser's throne, Edgar's face lights up. 'Impossivo. *Im*possivo. Imposs*ivo. Impossivo!'*

Everyone who speaks about Kaiser stresses his generosity of spirit, even if that sometimes strayed into calculated generosity. He was adept at subtly pressuring people to return a favour he had imposed upon them. 'I would often bump into Kaiser on nights out,' says the radio reporter Sergio Américo. 'I'd come in with my friends and he'd say, "Serginho, I've got a VIP area over there. Hang on, I'll get you a bracelet." He'd take you to the VIP section. Then he'd hug you and say, "Don't forget to mention on the radio tomorrow that Carlos Kaiser is going to be signing a contract with Botafogo."'

*** 

Kaiser loved to be the middleman, as it usually meant he would receive a thank-you from both sides. And while his name probably won't be found on the Fifa list of officially accredited player agents, he did tout some players around. He secured a trial at Botafogo for three beach soccer superstars, and another at the French club Montpellier for a striker called Paulo Dias. When his friend Luiz Maerovitch was looking for talented young players for a team that was affiliated to Fluminense, Kaiser made a number of recommendations. Most of them were not up to standard, and one day Maerovitch twigged what was going on. 'He was only recommending players whose mums were hot. I said to him, 'Is it the mum or her son who's going to play?''

\*\*\*

Dror Niv, the owner of the acclaimed sushi restaurant I Piatti, has served Kaiser many a free meal over the last thirty years. He has slowly learned how to read between the lies. 'Kaiser always tells a story with one objective: getting one over in some way,' he says. 'It's always for some reward. But what kind of reward depends on the circumstance.'

The reward was often food. Kaiser may have signed autographs as Renato Gaúcho but his signature was never seen on a restaurant cheque. There was a permanent hole in his pocket; he spent his money on everything from prostitutes to escorts. There were many days when he woke up with no money and no food, yet he hardly ever went hungry. 'I could be penniless,' he says, 'but if I had to take a girl out to dinner in the best place in Rio, I could.' There was always a little Brazilian way. The only question was how much dignity he would have to sacrifice.

Maerovitch remembers arriving at Porcão one evening when he saw Kaiser creating a scene at a corner table.

'I don't believe it!' shouted Kaiser to his female companion. 'Do you have a phone? Can you please lend me your phone?'

'What's wrong, Kaiser?'

'Please, can you lend me your phone?'

'But what's the problem?'

'What I did for America, the president is going to have to come here now.'

'But what?'

'With what I did for America, the president will have to come here and pay my bill.'

'Kaiser, I don't understand.'

'They gave me this credit card to use and there is no money on it! After all I have done for that bloody club!'

'Kaiser, it's okay, I'll pay. You can pay me back later.'

'That's not the point. It's humiliating. And I do not deserve to be treated like this. I score over thirty goals three seasons in a row and this is how they thank me.'

'Just let me pay.'

'Okay, you can pay for it but I'll pay you back tonight. This is unbelievable. This will never happen again.'

The woman paid the bill and left with Kaiser. That was one of many regular scams to ensure he didn't have to pay for anything. He hoofed ATMs in frustration as if they had swallowed his card, then sulked in the car until he was persuaded to allow his companion to pay for him. He also carried a chequebook with only one cheque left, which he would accidentally tear or sign incorrectly. That was a particular favourite at love motels. 'Can I settle up tomorrow? I'm a professional footballer, it's not like I'm going to do a runner. If I did you could just find me at the Maracanã!'

At one love motel he convinced the Portuguese owner that he had played for Braga in Portugal's Primeira Divisão, thus ensuring free rooms indefinitely. The owner was a Braga fan who was wowed by Kaiser's stories of playing alongside the Croatian hotshot Mladen Karoglan.

Maurício, the Botafogo star, noticed that whenever Kaiser accidentally bumped into him at the gym, it was just before lunchtime. Kaiser knew Maurício ate free at a nearby restaurant that was run by his father-in-law. 'We'd have lunch together,' laughs Maurício. 'He would eat up all his cheese and chicken. Good memories. Loads of cheese.'

The players liked having Kaiser around for lunch, even if they were paying, because they knew he would make them laugh until it hurt. Kaiser held court imperiously.

It was not so much the after-dinner circuit as the dinner circuit.

\*\*\*

Kaiser didn't jump queues; he ignored them. 'He never, ever paid to get into nightclubs,' says Fabinho. He was a self-made VIP who could gain access to anywhere in Rio. If Kaiser was not familiar with the bouncers he would show his ID card to ensure free entry. 'He was always flashing a card from a team in France,' says Tato. 'I can't remember if it was Bordeaux or Monaco. You'd look at the card and think, "It's possible that he played there." And he's pretty stylish too, so he looked the part.'

Kaiser had a card for every club, and therefore for every occasion. 'If it was an event only Fluminense players could get into, he would bring his Fluminense card,' says Maurício. 'Botafogo card, Vasco card, America card. He had cards from France, Italy and England. He had more cards than I did, and I was a Brazil international! There were places I couldn't get into but he would just walk in. He'd bring you straight to the VIP area where there were free drinks and free food. He would get you tickets for a Rolling Stones gig. And he would do so much promotion that when you got there everything would be at your fingertips.'

And you would be in his debt.

One day, Kaiser asked if he could borrow Maurício's car to take somebody out. As Kaiser did not have a driving licence and had spent the last week moaning about his declining eyesight, Maurício politely declined. Kaiser hatched another plan instead. He waited until it rained and turned up at the girl's house holding an umbrella. Kaiser was all apologies, explaining that his car was being repaired and that he didn't like driving his Honda CBR 1000 motorbike in the rain because he had nearly died in an accident a few years earlier. Then, as the taxi that had taken him there departed, Kaiser made a big song and dance about leaving his wallet in the back seat.

'That girl was drop-dead gorgeous and he went out with her as if nothing had happened,' says Maurício. 'She paid for everything – drinks, the taxis, the love motel, the lot. They had fun and danced the whole night. Only Kaiser would have those kinds of adventures. I wouldn't have the cheek but he's Kaiser. He's the man.'

\*\*\*

Carlos Alberto Torres decided it was time to find out if Kaiser really was the man. Kaiser was at his house, offering to get him a short-notice reservation in the blissful resort of Búzios for New Year's Eve. Carlos Alberto knew this was impossible even for him, the captain of the greatest team in football history. He was with his son Alexandre at the time and they decided to call Kaiser's bluff.

'Actually, I want to go! Sort it out because I want to come.'

'Oh, you want to go?'

'Yes.'

'Which day?'

'I want to spend New Year there. Let's say 30 December to 3 January.'

'Okay, can I use your phone? I just need to make a couple of calls.'

When Kaiser left the room, Carlos Alberto and his son laughed their heads off and started betting on the excuse he would come up with. Ten minutes later, there was still no sign of Kaiser. 'He's done a runner!' said Alexandre.

Soon after Kaiser came back in the room with details of Carlos Alberto's reservation. 'Just tell the manager I sent you, you'll be in the main suite.'

Carlos Alberto went to Búzios, half expecting to make the return journey a couple of hours later, but Kaiser's reservations held up. 'He stayed for five days,' says Alexandre. 'Anybody from Brazil knows that to get a hotel room in Búzios for five days over New Year's Eve is almost impossible. My dad, for example, would never think of asking somebody for something that he thought was out of reach. Kaiser was different. He goes and asks. He doesn't even ask, he demands it. And he gets it.'

\*\*\*

Kaiser was a pioneer of many things: player liaison, marketing, PR. And selling retro football shirts. It was one of his most reliable sources of income, or at least securing favours. He sold all kinds of shirts, many of them classics from the 1960s and 1970s, all of them fake. He also gave away replica shirts to restaurant owners. Leri Da Rosa, who owned Kaiser's favourite pizzeria, was thrilled to receive an original signed shirt from his hero, the former Paraguay and Grêmio defender Catalino Rivarola. Kaiser said he had played with Rivarola at Palmeiras. Da Rosa framed it in his lounge and cherished it until the day his son came to visit and pointed out it was a fake from a flea market.

Dror Niv, the owner of I Piatti, was given a signed shirt worn by Zico from the 1982 World Cup. 'Kaiser signed it himself!' he laughs. 'He would counterfeit everything and sell everything counterfeit.'

Sometimes, however, Kaiser did have authentic club shirts; it was just the backstory that came from a flea market. 'He asked those who played abroad to give him their team shirts, because he would take the shirt and claim he'd played there,' says Adriano Dias Oliveira. 'He had one from Nice in France. He also had a photo of him in a Paris Saint-Germain shirt, which meant he'd played there.'

The internet and globalisation have made it easy to buy almost any club shirt in the world, but in the twentieth century it was extremely difficult to find the kit of an overseas team. Kaiser's claims thus had a ring of truth.

Gil, the Botafogo manager, even gave him Kevin Keegan's shirt, which they swapped after Brazil's 1-1 draw at Wembley in 1978. Gil scored Brazil's goal in that game. As Kaiser was fourteen years old at the time, even he could not claim to have scored at Wembley.

\*\*\*

Renato Mendes Mota knew Kaiser was up to something; he just didn't know what it was. Why was Kaiser offering to pay for breakfast? And why, if Kaiser was paying, was he insisting they eat at the upmarket Spanish motel Viña del Mar? Mota was wearing a retro Barcelona training top, given to him by a friend who'd been there on holiday, and Kaiser said it was appropriate they should eat somewhere Spanish. 'But you should take the top off,' said Kaiser. 'It's a bit cheesy to walk in wearing that. Come on, man, show a bit of class.'

When they arrived, Kaiser walked confidently towards the reception.

'I'd like to speak with Mr Manolo, please.'

'Just a moment. Who should I say is here?'

'Carlos Henrique, the Botafogo footballer.'

After a couple of minutes, a short, rotund man arrived.

'Can I help you? I'm Manolo.'

'I'm Carlos Henrique, from Botafogo. You probably recognise me. This is my cousin Renato who plays for Flamengo and we'd like to have breakfast here. I wondered if I might also discuss something with you while we're here.'

Kaiser, Manolo and Mota started chatting over breakfast about their mutual love of Barcelona. After a couple of minutes, Kaiser looked at Mota and said, 'Renato, could you pass me my Barcelona top?'

Mota was nonplussed for a couple of seconds. Whose Barcelona top?

Those two seconds were all Kaiser needed.

'Listen,' he said, turning to Manolo, 'because you're a Barça fan I'm going to give you this Barcelona training top that I was given by Ricardo Bochini when I played for Independiente de la Plata in Argentina. It was given to him by Diego Maradona. Bochini was his idol. As a football connoisseur, I'm sure you know that.'

Manolo was still in a state of giddy gratitude when Kaiser got down to brass tacks. He said he and some of the other Botafogo players were looking for restaurant sponsorship.

Manolo got one of the staff to bring a packet of cards that allowed a fifty per cent discount in the restaurant with the fourth guest eating for free.

Kaiser used some of the cards for himself and sold the rest. 'He started to go to that hotel the whole time,' says Mota. 'They even allowed him to park in the hotel. This went on for a year until the cards ran out. Mr Manolo didn't renew the package.'

There were plenty of other packages. Valtinho, a mid-fielder who was with Kaiser at America, remembers him ostentatiously arriving at Toro, a BBQ restaurant, brandish-ing a footvolley trophy that Maurício had won, claiming it as his own and getting free lunches for a few months. He had an endless supply of free meals at steakhouses, pizzerias, fish restaurants, the lot. 'I remember one night in Leblon when we all ate for free and Kaiser signed as a famous Bangu player,' says Adriano. 'He would bark, "Put it on my tab." We ate, we drank and even went to a party afterwards, all thanks to Kaiser, who had no money in his pocket.'

Gustavo thought he and Kaiser were in trouble one day when, after another free lunch, a group of waiters and the manager awkwardly approached the table. They wanted Kaiser's autograph.

# CHAPTER 22

# THE ANIMAL

For most of his career Kaiser looked the part: slim, muscular, with barely an ounce of fat on him. But he had to work hard on his appearance. 'Kaiser was fucking fat when I met him,' says Alexandre Couto, his friend from Ajaccio. 'He weighed between a hundred and thirty and a hundred and forty kilos. He started dieting and working out, because for the character of Kaiser he needed to look like a footballer. I take my hat off to him.'

Kaiser's friends recall many extremes of dieting and eating down the years. 'He was like an animal,' says Fábio Braz, a Vasco defender who got to know Kaiser in the 2000s. 'I was shocked. I swear I've never seen somebody eat so much. He wasn't fat but he ate so much. Sometimes

I'd get embarrassed and say, "Calm down. Slow down." I don't know if he was taking some pill or something. He didn't mess around.'

Dror Niv has been serving Kaiser since the late 1980s and remembers everything from the days when Kaiser would only eat salad, through to his substantial Diet Coke addiction. 'There was a spell where he would only order this salad of chopped lettuce, tomato, cream cheese, parmesan and shredded chicken. He would order two of them. If the waiter only brought one and waited for him to finish until he started to make the second one, Kaiser would get really annoyed. He had to see both plates arrive in front of him at the same time.

'That was the same period as his Diet Coke phase. There's an all-night supermarket near where he lived. I've given him a lift home hundreds of times. He would buy a two-litre bottle of Diet Coke and a packet of biscuits. The bottle would go up, and it would not come down until it was empty. You wondered how it fit in his stomach.'

By befriending so many restaurant owners, Kaiser introduced the concept of the free all-you-can-eat meal – whether it was at Dror's seafood restaurant ('The Harumaki period') or Leri Da Rosa's pizzeria. On one occasion, Da Rosa and his colleagues decided to quantify Kaiser's appetite. He ate seventy miniature slices of pizza. 'Yeah, that's true,' sniffs Kaiser. 'I don't eat pizza anymore, though. It's not good for you.'

\*\*\*

The lack of family meant Kaiser usually spent Christmas with friends. One year he was invited to eat with his friend Cão and his family.

Cão's wife Fabiula lovingly laid the plates on the table and asked everyone to say grace. She put her hands together in prayer and was about to close her eyes when she noticed Kaiser's hand reaching tentatively for a plate of cheese.

'Kaiser, what are you doing?'

'Can I eat, Fabiula? I'm starving.'

'You're not a child. You have to say traditional graces. There's the shepherd's mass. You have to wait.'

'Just a little, Fabiula!'

'Bloody wait!'

'I just want one bit, I haven't eaten since yesterday!'

Kaiser had his cheese and then said grace with everyone else. For the next thirty minutes, while everyone savoured a beautiful, varied lunch, Kaiser systematically demolished a supply of cheese that was supposed to last Cão and Fabiula – and their children – until the new year.

Kaiser was banished, never to return; the Grinch who ate Christmas. The same happened another year at Alexandre

Couto's house. 'My mum made a big turkey,' he laughs. 'Everyone finished eating, and then Kaiser cleaned up all the leftovers. My mum was in shock. She liked him but after that she said, "That's it, he's not coming again. That was supposed to be going in the Tupperware."'

When Kaiser had to eat, he had to eat. Some of his proudest photos are taken from a dinner party at Carlos Alberto Torres's house. Maurício, Marcelo Campello and others are also there. In one photo, everyone is smiling at the camera – except Kaiser, who is face down in his food.

Kaiser's diets could be even more spectacular. Valtinho recalls the non-carbs phase, when Kaiser would shove ill-smelling protein shakes down his neck. Other times he would go out for dinner and just drink water, even if he wasn't paying.

Kaiser has an alternative explanation for the youthful weight gain that his friends found so amusing. 'Do they know that they injected corticoid in my groin because I said I had an injury, and that they fucked it up so badly that it affected my metabolism?' he says. 'That's why I put on so much weight.'

\*\*\*

When Renato Gaúcho went to Cruzeiro in 1992, Kaiser decided to tag along for a few weeks. They were coached by Jair Pereira, who had won everything in Brazil, as well as an Under-20 World Cup with his country and the Copa del Rey while at the Spanish giants Atlético Madrid. The list of geniuses he managed includes Júnior, Bernd Schuster, Paulo Futre and Renato Gaúcho. It's not hard to imagine what he made of Kaiser's first touch.

'He was very skilful,' says Pereira, to widespread astonishment. The first time the two met, he says, Kaiser flicked the ball up and controlled it on the back of his neck. 'He had amazing skill. He didn't pass through all those teams just by being charming. I got to see him train. He was in good shape. He had a good shot on him.'

# CHAPTER 23

# THE TV STAR

In October 1991, the Rio newspaper *O Dia* published a story entitled 'The Jobless Team'. It was about Professionals United, a group of thirty-five players without a club and looking to return to elite football. They were playing a series of training matches against Rio clubs, including Vasco da Gama and Bangu. The story tells of three 'notable recruits' who had joined the team in the previous few days. One was Mongol, the centre-back who won the Campeonato Carioca with Botafogo in 1989. Then there was Luisinho, a former America player who also had a spell in Portugal with Filgueiras. You might recognise the third player.

*'Carlos Kayser (sic), 28 years old, started in the youth team at Botafogo ... he went to Puebla where he turned*

*professional and then ended up at Independiente in Argentina when he became Libertadores and World Champion in 1984. Now his pass belongs to Ajaccio of Corsica, in the French second division:*

*"'I'm ok financially and my aim is to help the group. I'm friends with the agent, Frank Henouda, who has some dealings in the USA, and while I'm with the group I'll be evaluating the players to find work for the ones who most impress.'"*

The feature was accompanied by a big picture of the players sprawled across a kerb. The most prominent was Kaiser, sat front and centre, looking like the star of the group.

\*\*\*

The longer he spent in the world of football, the more Kaiser started to understand how the media worked – and the more confident he became about manipulating it. The printed word had authority, even in such an oral culture, and whether it was true or not was largely irrelevant. 'Once Kaiser's lies were published once, he kept on telling them and people kept on publishing them,' says the journalist Martha Esteves. 'They became the truth.'

He befriended journalists, particularly those whose standards were less than rigorous, and gently persuaded them to write articles about him. Some fell for his lies; others knew he was spinning a mixture of truth and fiction, but he made it worth their while to write his story.

Life is an exchange. Kaiser offered incentives from the professional (setting up interviews with famous players, off-the-record scoops) to the personal (VIP access at nightclubs, goodness knows what else). 'I had so much clout with the press that nobody exposed me,' says Kaiser. 'I kept everybody sweet, whether it was the players or journalists for the biggest newspapers. They wanted to talk with the players and I made that happen.'

The articles reinforced Kaiser's backstory, while excluding minor details like the fact he was a centre-forward who couldn't remember his last goal. They also contained comical flights of fancy and, most brazenly of all, those gratuitous references to his single status.

Esteves, who has covered Brazilian football for over thirty years, never wrote an article about Kaiser but can sympathise with those who did. 'He was a storyteller and people fell for it,' she says. 'It might have been on a slow news day where there was some space in the newspaper. Then some player turns up saying he played in France. We didn't have access to the kind of information we have in today's globalised world, with Google and YouTube. It was easier to be fooled – not just journalists but fans and directors as well.

'With some of the articles it's obvious the journalist hasn't verified the details. The newspapers didn't have enough money to call places like France or Mexico. Nowadays it would be impossible for somebody to fall for his stories, even an intern. Back then journalists often didn't have degrees and some had to work in three, four, five places. Salaries were small and life was tough.'

Despite that, Esteves does not believe there was an overt bribe for publishing articles about Kaiser. 'I suspect they were done in exchange for a favour. Since he was such a big mouth, he could say he would introduce them to Roberto Baggio or some famous French player. I definitely don't believe he paid them. For a start, he didn't have any money.'

\*\*\*

When Kaiser saw a teenager handing out free newspapers on Pepe Beach, he grabbed a copy and searched for details of how to contact the editorial department. He introduced himself as the former Independiente player Carlos Henrique and persuaded them to publish a Q&A: name, age, favourite food, favourite music, teams. It was accompanied by the old picture of Kaiser in his Ajaccio shirt.

A week later, again on Pepe Beach, Renato Mendes Mota was lounging around in a group that included Kaiser.

'I wondered what he was doing,' says Renato. 'He called over two kids, paid them a bit of money and said, "Listen, you're going to give away copies of this paper only to the hot girls on the beach. And as you deliver it, you're going to point over to me. I'm going to be up here by the kiosk. Deliver the papers to the girls then point to me." The kids delivered over a hundred copies of that newspaper on Pepe Beach.'

\*\*\*

Adriano Dias Oliveira was channel-hopping one night when he froze. He did a triple take, looked back at his TV screen and it still showed his friend Kaiser. On the biggest football show in Rio.

Kaiser had talked his way onto the football show *Mesa Redonda*, holding court in one of the seats usually reserved for the elite of Brazilian football.

José Carlos Araújo, who co-presented the show with Washington Rodrigues, struggles to recall Kaiser's appearance. 'I don't remember that character. Is there a video?'

There is a video, which has pride of place in Kaiser's collection.

'I'll explain why I don't remember,' says Araújo. 'These characters were often brought along by a friend or a player.

There was no other way he'd get on the show. What a character! If a proposal like that came to us nowadays, we'd go on Google and investigate. Back then there wasn't that kind of resource so we would get people recommended to us. He must have a good press agent.'

Kaiser had a great press agent: himself. His memory of how his appearance came about is slightly different. Araújo celebrated his wedding anniversary at Maxim's nightclub, where Kaiser was the PR manager. Kaiser plied him with free champagne and then popped the question: could he come on *Mesa Redonda*? In his rendered state, Araújo gave Kaiser his word.

Kaiser went on *Mesa Redonda* looking sharp, in a blazer and pleated shirt. He presented Araújo and Rodrigues with one of his Ajaccio tops. The panel discussed the weekend's football in the usual style before moving on to the subject of what it was like to play in France. And then – on national TV, on the biggest football show in Brazil – Kaiser looked straight to camera and told the story of the female gift he received upon arriving at Ajaccio. As he delivered the punchline – 'I told her, "When the pitch is flooded I shoot from behind the goal"' – the panel collapsed in laddish hysterics.

Kaiser made a second appearance a few years later, when he was invited to nominate the Goal of the Week, the prize for which was a VW Golf. Kaiser surprised everyone by ignoring a stunning bicycle kick from Marcelinho Carioca and giving the award to Edmundo. 'I thought Marcelinho Carioca's goal was better,' says Kaiser. 'I'm not stupid. But Edmundo was a brother to me. I think it was the second car he ever owned.'

# CHAPTER 24

# THE DECENT SCOUNDREL

It was just another footballer lunch: Alexandre Torres and Ricardo Rocha, Brazilian internationals, and Carlos Kaiser. They had convened at a buffet, and Kaiser was determinedly overcoming a plate of chicken when a woman walked over to say hello to Torres. After a couple of minutes' small talk she left. As soon as she was out of earshot, Kaiser asked for an introduction.

'Come on, Kaiser. She's my bank manager. I don't know her well enough. I'm her customer but I'm not a friend of hers.'

'Fine, leave it to me.'

Kaiser sidled over to the buffet, returning with another plate of chicken and a phone number.

'How, man? That was so quick!'

'I went over and said I was a footballer just returning from Italy and that I needed to invest all the money I'd earned abroad in her bank.'

Like all actors, much of Kaiser's best work was unscripted and improvised. He gathered an encyclopaedia's worth of information but rarely wrote anything down. He had a memory that would make an elephant question itself. And while some of his tall tales were pre-planned, the majority were reactions to the requirements of the moment.

'He goes wherever the tide takes him,' says Ricardo Rocha. 'Back and forth. If it was fashionable to be a witch doctor he would become one. He'd do anything.'

And he does it with total conviction. 'He would say to me, "If I don't believe the lie I'm telling, who else is going to believe it?"' says Renato Mendes Mota. 'And he would usually have a comeback for any negative response.'

Most of Kaiser's tricks would not have worked had he not been so charismatic and likeable. Everyone goes out of their way to say he was a good 171 – your friendly neighbourhood con man, who they loved for his big heart and even bigger hair. 'Kaiser is cool in every sense of the word,' said Carlos Alberto Torres. 'He's a guy that puts loyalty above all else. I don't know of anybody who has a story showing Kaiser as untrustworthy. He charmed everybody around him.'

Kaiser's abnormal memory allowed him to make a series of small, thoughtful gestures. If somebody arrived late to meet him, a glass of their favourite beer would be waiting. (Though it would almost certainly be on their tab.) He found out what team a person supported or what toys their child liked and gave gifts accordingly. And then there were the familiar social perks. 'He takes you to the best places and he's always surrounded by beautiful women,' says Edgar Pereira. 'Who wouldn't want a friend like that?'

That ability to store so much detail was one of Kaiser's greatest strengths. 'He has an incredible memory, and he's a very intelligent guy,' says Alexandre Couto. 'He gathers information then creates a story and saves it in his "natural HD".'

The amorality of Kaiser's behaviour did not bother most people. This was Rio, where everyone had to find their own way to survive. 'Kaiser is a decent scoundrel,' says Júnior Negão. 'He was full of tricks but they were never nasty and he's not a malevolent guy. I never heard of him doing wrong by anybody. He was just kind of dodgy in a good way. I've never heard anyone say they don't like Kaiser. Everybody liked him because of his whole picaresque rascal vibe.'

Renato Gaúcho had more reason than most to dislike Kaiser, who regularly stole his identity, yet he will not hear a word against him. 'Kaiser's a decent 171, which is very rare in Brazil, because he never wanted to screw anybody over,' he says. 'That is something to be admired. And whenever he could help somebody out, he would. That's a great quality of his. I know that if somebody hates Kaiser, it's because that person doesn't like themselves. They're on the wrong planet. The whole world is wrong for that person if they don't like Kaiser.'

What Renato doesn't know is that Zico, his idol and friend, is among the small group who do not see the good in Kaiser's story. 'A 171 is a scam artist, who sells something he doesn't have,' says Zico. 'They're always bad.' Although there is that photo of Zico with Kaiser, taken at the Brazilian team hotel before the 1986 World Cup, he does not remember him. 'The only Kaiser I know is Beckenbauer! I think it's sad that a person lives like that. We humans are all different. I think he's an affront to the profession of football. No, he's a complete liar. You can't call that a career. How can you have a career if you didn't play?'

\*\*\*

Kaiser marketed himself at every opportunity. He was one of the first Brazilian footballers to own a mobile phone, which he used constantly at Botafogo. It was the size of a brick, and Kaiser's use of it was about as a subtle as a brick through a window. He ostentatiously negotiated his next date or his next transfer. One morning, after training, Kaiser asked for some decorum.

'Can you peasants shut up, please? Josep Lluís Núñez is due to call me in a second.'

A couple of players asked who he was.

'He's the president of Barcelona! You lot are so ignorant.'

'Why's he calling you?'

'Johan Cruyff wants to sign a Brazilian to play alongside Michael Laudrup and Hristo Stoichkov.'

Right on cue, Kaiser's phone started to ring. As he answered, the players all started hollering in mock excitement.

'Señor Núñez, can I call you back in an hour, we have just finished training.'

Kaiser pressed a button and put the phone in his bag.

'You lot have no class,' he sniffed, before undressing and walking into the shower.

One player asked why Kaiser needed a shower when all he'd done was stand around all morning. Another wondered why he was speaking to the president of Barcelona in Portuguese. At this point, Nelson decided to have a rummage through Kaiser's bag. He pulled out the phone, pressed a couple of buttons and placed it to his ear. Nothing. It was a toy phone.

\*\*\*

Botafogo were Rio champions again in 1990 and also lost in the Brazilian championship final of 1992. Then things started to unravel. There were a number of financial scandals in Brazilian football at the time, including at Botafogo. A director was caught embezzling funds from the club, and though Emil Pinheiro was not involved – he was so wealthy that he had no need to steal from the club – he was implicated and resigned.

It got worse. Denise Frossard, a judge, sent fourteen *bicheiros* to prison in 1993, including Pinheiro and Castor de Andrade. When the police raided de Andrade's accounts and computers, they found half of Rio was on his payroll – including the former president, the governor and the mayor, as well as judges, congressmen, assemblymen, twenty-five police commissioners and a hundred police officers. De Andrade died in 1997, when his funeral was openly attended by many Brazilian football greats. Pinheiro died in 2001.

When Pinheiro left Botafogo, Kaiser stopped organising orgies and found himself a new role. He fabricated the necessary certificate and started a water aerobics class at the club's Mourisco headquarters.

It went extremely well, most of the time. Kaiser had recently started seeing a tall, blonde girl, whose ex-boyfriend arrived one day and gave Kaiser an unsolicited right-hander in front of his hydro-gym class. As he was being dragged towards the back door by a couple of heavies, the man shouted to anyone who would listen: 'He's a fucking 171! He shouldn't be at Botafogo! You should fire him!'

Kaiser, surrounded by concerned pupils in dental-floss bikinis, gingerly touched his cheekbone. 'What was that guy's problem?' asked someone.

'I've no idea,' said Kaiser. 'I think he got me mixed up with someone else.'

Soon after, Kaiser persuaded a young journalist at *Jornal da Zona Sul* to publish a feature about his career sideline.

*'The footballer Carlos Henrique is giving hydro-gym-nastic classes and presenting a sports show* Real Strong *while waiting for the French club Ajaccio to formally release him ... The player has one foot abroad and one in Brazil. Kayzer [sic] was selected to play in Arabia, but the negotiations have stalled. The player has tried several times to get in touch with the French club but they hav-en't responded.*

*"'If I go to Arabia now it would just be running away because loving somebody so much has made football trickier for me and now I couldn't do that," stated the Ajaccio legend, who is going through an emotionally difficult period. If the player doesn't go to Arabia, he will stay in Brazil as a football agent.'*

# CHAPTER 25

# THE KING OF BEERS

When the 1994 World Cup was awarded to the USA, the average American knew very little about football. This was a situation Kaiser was only too happy to exploit. The beer company Budweiser wanted to film an advert in Brazil, which anyone with even a passing knowledge of the game knew was the home of football. Their marketing team contacted Fluminense and were eventually put in touch with the club's fitness coach, Kaiser's old friend Marcelo Campello.

They asked if he could arrange a group of players for the advert and stressed one caveat: they needed to be photogenic. If there was one person who knew how to *look* the part, it was Kaiser. Everyone was paid $1,000, whether they appeared in the advert or not, which was sufficient incentive for Kaiser. 'They must have paid him bloody well to get up so early every day,' says Joel Santana, the coach, who was hired as a consultant and coordinator. Kaiser may have been teetotal, but he had a certain moral flexibility when it came to promoting alcohol. Besides, who better to appear in an advert for the King of Beers than a man named Kaiser?

The advert involved long days, from dawn till beyond dusk, and Kaiser filled much of the time by chatting up the director. 'He must have spoken English really well because she couldn't speak Portuguese,' says Santana. 'Or he was talking in a different dialect. He ended up showing her around Rio. They got very well acquainted. I think a romance could well have happened there. I can't confirm it but I know they were very close.'

While Kaiser may have been photogenic, he proved to be unusually camera-shy. His desperation to avoid the ball was such that he was almost always out of shot. One part of the advert required a player to leap triumphantly and head the ball. Even Kaiser could manage that. As he did so, his mullet wafted imperiously across his face. He could have been in a shampoo advert. It was the only thing of note that anyone saw Kaiser do throughout filming – and it ended up in a commercial that was watched by millions across America during the World Cup.

When he is reminded of the advert, the star striker Bebeto bursts out laughing. 'Bloody hell!' he says. 'I remember that. And they put him in the advert! That's what I'm saying: if you let that lad open his mouth, it's over. People who didn't know him thought he was an idol. Man, they actually chose Kaiser. Unbelievable.'

\*\*\*

Brazil started the 1994 World Cup being criticised for their style of play and ended it the same way – even though they won the competition. The coach Carlos Alberto Parreira, like Sebastião Lazaroni in 1990, placed a greater emphasis on defence, with a back four and two holding midfielders in Dunga and Mauro Silva. All he wanted to do was end a twenty-four-year wait for the World Cup – still Brazil's longest drought since their first victory in 1958. Brazil were dangerously dependent on the attacking brilliance of their strikers, Romário and Bebeto. 'We had a nice team and a great spirit,' says the defender Ricardo Rocha, 'but without those two we wouldn't have won the World Cup.'

'It was the best partnership I had in football,' says Bebeto. 'A gift from God. I think it was one of the best in Brazilian football history. Everybody knows the story of Bebeto and Romário. I had the pleasure of playing with him.'

A number of the team, including Romário and Bebeto, had been part of the 1990 squad that was savaged after losing to Argentina in the second round. 'We stuck together really tightly because of the hurt of 1990,' says Ricardo Rocha. 'You learn a lot more in life through losing than winning. We were written off in 1994 but the group was very unified and tough, which was crucial in winning that World Cup.'

The tournament started six weeks after the death of the Formula 1 genius Ayrton Senna, which had a devastating impact on the morale of the country. 'The public really needed something to cheer about,' says Bebeto. 'Brazilian people have to go through a lot. They're really resilient, hard-working people. We wanted to bring joy to them. Everybody put their egos aside. When the president came to talk about money we said to him, "We don't care how much you are going to pay us, what matters to us is winning this tournament." That was a really important moment. We had a shared purpose. I shared a room with Zinho, and we'd say to each other, "Let's do this, man!"'

Brazil rarely hit the attacking heights, despite the obvious brilliance of Romário and Bebeto, and scored only five goals in the four knockout games. The first of those was a tough 1-0 win over the hosts, on Independence Day. 'It was the fourth of July,' says Ricardo Rocha, 'it was fifty degrees – and then we had ten men.' Leonardo, the mild-mannered, urbane left-back, was sent off for a vicious elbow that fractured the skull of the American Tab Ramos. 'Leonardo was never violent,' says Ricardo Rocha. 'He was a really technical player. The image is horrible but he was trying to shake him off with an elbow to the ribs, not the face.'

Brazil then beat Holland 3-2 in the quarter-finals, a minor classic that included the first demonstration of Bebeto's iconic baby-rocking celebration, and was eventually settled by a ferocious free-kick from Kaiser's friend Branco. They then crept past Sweden 1-0 in the semi-finals thanks to a late goal from the inevitable Romário. He was so keen to win the competition that he broke the habit of a lifetime and trained vigorously the day before the final – so much so that he felt severe muscular pain and almost missed the match.

The final against Italy was a poor game, a weary 0-0 draw. It was the first World Cup final to go to penalties. The most memorable moment came in extra-time: a solo run of bewildering brilliance by the substitute Viola, who beat six players before setting up Romário for a shot that was desperately blocked. Few people outside Brazilian football had heard of him before the match; nor would they hear about him again. It was another reminder of the extraordinary depth of talent in Brazilian football.

Brazil won the penalty competition 4-2, with Roberto Baggio famously missing the final kick. It was a bitter-sweet experience for Kaiser. A few months earlier he was at Caligula when he met an Italian tourist called Marina. She was a Buddhist, a culture that had always interested Kaiser; and a cousin of the Italian legend Baggio, which definitely interested Kaiser. The similarities between Italian and Corsican allowed Marina and Kaiser to communicate easily, and their holiday romance was such that she asked him to go back to Europe with her. Kaiser did not want to leave Rio permanently but did spend time in Turin, where he met Baggio and started to discover more about Buddhism. When he returned to Rio, Kaiser decided to embrace the culture fully.

'It was difficult for me to see him miss, even though my country became world champions,' says Kaiser. 'For any Buddhist to see somebody who lives their life being kind to their neighbour being condemned by a nation because they missed a penalty. He didn't deserve that. He aged really fast. If you look at Baggio, he went grey very early. I put myself in his shoes and felt his suffering.'

The victory was cathartic for a team that had been the subject of criticism from their own media in particular. When the captain Dunga lifted the trophy, he shouted 'This is for you, you treacherous bastards! What do you say now?'

The criticism of Brazil's style – before, during and after the tournament – came mainly from the press. 'I don't think it was a great team,' says Martha Esteves. 'But we won. Even if it was on penalties, we won. Brazilian supporters like victory. I remember the 1982 and 1986 teams with a lot more passion, but most Brazilian supporters prefer to remember the 1994 squad, because although they played ugly, they won.'

Even more importantly, they won for the first time since 1970. 'The public were a little impatient so that restored peace to Brazilian football,' says Ricardo Rocha. 'It had been a long time. Brazilians ended up admiring that discredited national team who clawed their way back after 1990. After so long without a World Cup, Brazilian football unburdened itself.'

As in 1990, the players couldn't walk the streets when they returned from the World Cup. This time, it was for the right reasons. 'When we returned it was so moving,' says Bebeto. 'The first place we came back to was Recife. The image of when we passed Boa Viagem Beach will never leave me. Our plane had the Brazilian colours on it. Everybody was on the beach and I was at the window seat. Then I saw the crowd. That's priceless. I'm getting goosebumps now. It was so joyful. It's hard to grasp the scale of it.'

Though the criticism of the team's style was fair enough – they were Brazil in name rather than nature – they did not receive enough credit for the authority of their World Cup win. They were easily the best team in the tournament and played with a formidable certainty. You always felt they were in control: even when they went down to ten men in the first half against the USA, even when Holland came back from 2-0 down to equalise in the quarter-final, even when the final against Italy went to the supposed lottery of penalties. Few World Cup winners have had such an obvious sense of destiny.

\*\*\*

The World Cup confirmed Romário as one of the greatest goalscorers in football history. At 5ft 5ins he benefited from a lack of size: he had a sprinter's ability to explode from a standing start and the capacity to change direction in tight areas. 'He was the best striker I played against,' says Ricardo Rocha. 'I've never seen another player like him. Johan Cruyff said he was the king of the penalty box.' Romário was indecently cool in front of goal and has a strong case for being the greatest one-on-one finisher of all time. He's certainly the one with the greatest flair, imagination and arrogance.

Some people think a one-on-one is about scoring or saving a goal. For Romário, the one-on-one was a power game, a masculinity-waving contest. It was also a fascinating puzzle, and he found some ingenious ways – little Brazilian ways – to score. He could scoop, lob or chip. He could toe-poke it in. He could nutmeg the keeper. His favourite trick was to dance cockily, effortlessly round the keeper; sometimes he would do that and then do it again. Romário loved humiliating goalkeepers, the favelado showing everyone who was boss.

When Romário lived on the top floor of a posh condominium in Barra, he regularly held all-night parties to the exasperation of his neighbours. Every clockwise twist of the volume dial was designed to say: I'm a favelado, and I live here now, what are you going to do about it? 'The more prejudice there was against him, the more he would do it,' says Martha Esteves. 'It was the same on the pitch.'

He was an irresistible ball of charisma who said and did what he wanted. When he was asked by a magazine to give some life tips, the list included:

'Find a prick to slag you off and motivate yourself with this challenge.'

'Dream like fuck.'

'Shag every day, three times at the most.'

Romário was a poster boy for unprofessionalism – he loved nightclubs and felt he played better if he had been out the night before a match, although he was at least teetotal. 'I don't smoke,' he said once. 'I don't drink, I don't use drugs, but women …'

The TV presenter Washington Rodrigues says Romário's penis was known as 'the lethal weapon'. He got to know him well, especially when he unexpectedly became Flamengo manager in 1995. 'Romário is an amazing character, but you have to understand the man. He would go to bed at 7 p.m., wake up at 1 a.m. and have nothing to do, so he'd go to a nightclub. Barring Pelé, who is immortal, Romário was the best Brazilian attacker I've seen. Of the mortals, it's Romário without a doubt. He wasn't tall or athletic, he didn't like training. But he loved playing. Romário knew all the shortcuts. He was so good at finding space.'

Like so many of his generation, Romário lived fast and, in football terms, died old. He played until he was forty-three. His lifestyle didn't do him too much harm.

# CHAPTER 26

# THE SUIT

During the World Cup, Kaiser finally negotiated a permanent departure from Ajaccio. He hadn't actually been to Corsica for years but was thrilled to cut the last bit of red tape. The day before the World Cup final, Ajaccio renamed the Stade Mezzavia. It would now be called Stade Ange Casanova, in memory of a former director of the club. When he saw the name Casanova, Kaiser assumed it was a tribute to him.

He was even prouder when he saw his name in *Jornal dos Sports*, the highbrow Rio newspaper. 'The headline is there for anyone who wants to see it,' he says. '"BANGU HAS ITS KING." Who's that, Zizinho? Joe Bloggs? No, Carlos Kaiser.'

Brazil's victory at the World Cup replenished Kaiser's enthusiasm for impersonating a footballer, and he returned to Bangu after leaving Ajaccio. He signed a three-month contract which, by coincidence, was officially witnessed by Mario Barros, the brother of his old Ajaccio team-mate Fabinho.

When Carlos Alberto Torres read about Kaiser in *Jornal dos Sports*, it made his day. 'I was genuinely shocked when I read it,' he says. 'But it's that thing of being shocked but also rooting for it to be true and for him to be happy.'

The *Jornal dos Sports* article, searching for a synonym of 'journeyman' to describe Kaiser's career, called him a 'gypsy highness'. With the volume of football coverage starting to increase, there was even more opportunity for Kaiser to get his name in print.

\*\*\*

Kaiser occasionally joined in training while at Bangu, where the lower standard was more to his taste, but did not play a game. When his contract expired, the tide took him to America, the small club at which he had a spell in the mid-eighties. This time there was no pretence of football-related activity. He asked his friend Valtinho to arrange a meeting with the coach Luisinho. 'I'm not going to play,' said Kaiser to Valtinho. 'I'm going to be on the books so I can operate in the environment I'm familiar with. Playing would be difficult.'

Luisinho was an America legend, the leading goalscorer in the club's history with 311. He had a slight doubt as to whether Kaiser was good enough to play for the club.

'Come on, Valtinho, Kaiser's shite. How am I going to get him to play here?'

'He doesn't want to play – he just wants to be around the club and sort some sponsorship. Trust me, he is a genius at that kind of thing.'

'Okay, I'll see what I can do. But he's not playing.'

Luisinho arranged for Kaiser to meet the club president, Francisco Cantizano, on a Thursday afternoon. What he knew – and Kaiser didn't – was that Cantizano saw nobody on Thursdays. The day was reserved for members' parties and a lunch so long that it doubled up as dinner.

The next morning, Kaiser breezed into training and said hello to Luisinho.

'Kaiser, can you wait until you've spoken to the president before you come to training?'

'Oh, that's okay, I saw him yesterday – he signed my contract.'

Kaiser produced his new America contract, lest there be any doubt. Valtinho says he still has no idea how Kaiser did it. But he fulfilled his promise of sponsorship, setting up a major deal with a brand called Waterproof.

They supplied all the players with watches, caps, towels, beach bats and other surfing gear. You didn't necessarily have to be at America to benefit, either. He got Maurício, an Internacional player at the time, a sponsorship with Waterproof and a supermarket sweep at Cantão.

'I was allowed to go in the shop and take whatever I liked so long as I wore it in interviews,' says Maurício. 'Kaiser was a pioneer of product placement within football. It's normal these days. He had that perceptiveness years back.'

Kaiser also sorted out unofficial sponsorships at various restaurants for the players. In return, he was allowed to sit on the bench for each game, in his full kit, to all intents and purposes just another footballer.

In some ways this was Kaiser's imperial phase, when he discovered weird and wonderful ways to appear in newspapers. In 1995, he took on the might of Greenpeace – and trounced them. A group of seventeen activists had chained themselves to the entrance of the French consulate in a protest against nuclear testing. The initial reaction of the security guard was to point a gun at all of them, until he was made aware of the concept of the peaceful protest.

The ensuing standoff meant nobody was able to receive travel visas, no matter how urgent. As word spread of the protest, Kaiser sensed another opportunity to get himself in the news. He decided he had not left Ajaccio after all and swanned over to the consulate to renew his imaginary visa. What happened next was told in a local newspaper the next day:

*'The consulate decided to keep the doors closed and the deadlock remained until the arrival of a strapping gentleman in sunglasses, cap and dungarees, who was unhappy at the controlled irritation of the customs brokers. He quickly assessed the situation and said, "Let's get these guys out of the way". Immediately the group went on the attack and a protest that had lasted five hours was dispersed in five minutes. "I have to travel today and I can't tolerate this nonsense," stated the man in question – Carlos Kaiser, Carioca, 32 years, ex-Vasco, ex-Bangu and current player for Ajaccio, who play in the French second division.'*

A few weeks later, Kaiser was in the news again.

*'After playing for several teams in Rio, among them Vasco, Botafogo, Bangu and America, and playing abroad, the centre-forward and right midfielder Carlos Henrique Kayzer is temporarily going from the football pitch to the Muay Thai ring. Ready for success in martial arts, on 27th July in the Comary Club in Teresopolis, Carlos will challenge the reigning Brazilian middle weight (79 to 85kg) champion through the amateur Thai boxing association – Naja – whose president and world light middle weight champion, Wellington Narany, is his trainer.*

'Being contractually beholden to Ajaccio, a French second division club, the player has been training for four months to compete for his first title since he became a black belt in Muay Thai, having been a student of professor Alesandro, in Ibeas Top Club.

'He guarantees however that, even winning the Brazilian title and going on to other victories, he has no intention of abandoning the green grass of football and he's even hoping to settle a contract with a club in order to play in the Brazilian Championship. Last year, Carlinhos played for America, then managed by Luisinho, vying for a place with Andre Luiz.'

Never mind Muay Thai: Kaiser was a black belt in barefaced lying.

# CHAPTER 27

# THE KING OF RIO

By January 1995, Romário was the best player in the world. He had just won the Fifa Player of the Year award, getting more votes than everyone else combined, and would have claimed the Ballon d'Or had he been eligible. (It was not until the following year that non-European players could win the award.) *L'Equipe*, the celebrated French newspaper, even gave him their all-sport Champion of Champions award for 1994, an honour won previously by, among others, Carl Lewis, Ayrton Senna and Michael Jordan.

It was, all things considered, a major story when he decided he wanted to leave Barcelona and join Flamengo. At a time when almost everybody else was going in the opposite direction, it gave Brazilian domestic football – and especially Rio football – a huge boost. It also sparked one of the most famous seasons in the history of the Campeonato Carioca: the battle to determine the King of Rio. When people bemoan the lack of glamour and personality in the modern domestic game, it is years such as 1995 that they have in mind.

There were three formal contenders for the crown. Romário represented Flamengo; Renato Gaúcho was with Fluminense; and Túlio Maravilha was at Botafogo. The season was a memorable mix of brilliance on the field and largely playful trash talk off it. It was elite football with all the pantomime drama of WWE.

The 1990s was a new era in Brazilian domestic football, especially in Rio. The quiet achievement of players like Zico and Júnior, the stars of Flamengo's 1980s team, was exchanged for the kind of brazen showmanship pioneered by Renato Gaúcho.

The playful nature of the rivalry was typical of Rio; even in purely football terms, it often felt like a separate country rather than a separate state. 'I have the impression that in the south – where Dunga is from, for example – the culture is very different,' says the journalist Martha Esteves. 'It's a lot harder and more serious. The players are bigger. In Rio it's lighter, faster and more dynamic.'

Romário and Edmundo represented a new type of Brazilian star: the bad boy. 'Every team had somebody who would provoke the opposition,' says Esteves. 'It wasn't necessarily a movement of bad boys: they were just individually cunts. They were rebels with no cause. They were people who came from poor backgrounds and weren't psychologically or socially prepared to deal with fame. They did what they wanted. I think it was around then that the players started seeing the press as the enemy, especially if they did something off the pitch and the press published it.'

Esteves first interviewed Romário when he was nineteen and had just been promoted to Vasco's first team. 'He'd just left the favela,' she says. 'He was shy and didn't know how to deal with the press. He was engaged to Monica, who was fifteen then. At that time he was very approachable. I liked him, he was a nice guy. I think the big change was when he had a crisis in his marriage and started turning into a different person, and also when he became a really big player. That's when he started to put on the bad-boy attitude.'

There is footage of Romário, shot by a Dutch TV station when he was a PSV Eindhoven player, idly fiddling with a handgun on Copacabana Beach. The whole thing was staged, but it's not hard to imagine how such images would be received in the modern world.

Romário and Edmundo were great friends, and their image was so strong that they even recorded a funk/rap song called 'Bad Boys'. They both had a rap sheet, too, with a long list of misdemeanours from the sporting to the criminal. Edmundo's included feeding beer to a chimp at his son's birthday party; smashing a TV camera during a game in Ecuador and locking himself in a hotel room for three days to avoid being nicked; a 120-day ban for slapping a referee; having it written into his contract at the Italian club Fiorentina that he could go to nightclubs. And a fatal car crash in 1995, when three people were killed. Edmundo was eventually convicted of manslaughter but only spent one night in jail before being released pending appeal. The appeals dragged on until 2007, when the statute of limitations expired.

Romário's list includes beating up a Fluminense fan who threw chickens at the team during a training session; urinating on pedestrians from a hotel window, for which he was dropped from the Brazil youth team; and even threatening to pull out of USA 94 if he didn't get a window seat on the flight over.

Edmundo and Romário had a thundering fallout in 2000, when both were playing for Vasco. The speculation as to why it happened ranges from a row over who should be club captain to an alleged threesome gone wrong.

Renato Gaúcho and Túlio did not quite fit the bad-boy profile. They craved publicity but achieved it in different ways – by appearing in soap operas as more extreme versions of themselves, on TV shows as more extreme versions of themselves, or on the football field as more extreme versions of themselves. Túlio also posed naked for G, a Brazilian gay magazine, a bold thing to do in the most macho area of an already homophobic culture.

'Túlio was brilliant with the media,' says Martha Esteves. 'He wasn't a womaniser, he just had a big mouth. He was a mediocre footballer, but he scored a load of goals. He created this incredible character of himself, and he embodied that character so much that he still doesn't know who Túlio is. He speaks about himself in the third person.'

When Túlio was involved in a very public love triangle involving his wife and a prostitute, Esteves started to publish a Túlio soap opera in the magazine *Placar*. 'He even got involved!' she laughs. 'He liked it. Nowadays I'd never dream of doing that. I'd get sued. I'd be harassed or threatened. You'll never get a player like Túlio nowadays. They just say something boring.'

Túlio was a goal machine (even if his claim to have scored over 1,000 goals in his career might be stretching it) and in 1995 he top-scored in both the Brazilian league and the Campeonato Carioca. His character made him perfect for such a rivalry.

'There's another funny story about Túlio,' says Esteves. 'When he retired he went to Sport TV, Globo's channel, where they invited him to be a pundit. Then he went to present a show, and before going live he showed a picture of himself naked with a boner to his fellow presenter. It's because he did a naked thing for a gay magazine back in the day, so he wanted to show her he was still on form. After that, Globo didn't show him on anything.'

\*\*\*

When he heard that Valtinho and Romário, senior players at America and Flamengo respectively, were due to meet Marcello Alencar, the governor of Rio, Kaiser decided he could be of use. In those days, wages were partly linked to ticket sales and some imperfect accounting meant the players were being short-changed. Valtinho and Romário arrived to find Kaiser waiting for them, rambling on about what an important cause it was to him and how he wanted to be part of discussions. He was even wearing a suit, which he had borrowed from his next-door neighbour.

When Valtinho and Romário reached the governor's office they told Kaiser he had to wait outside. He faked outrage but didn't mind one bit. There were no paparazzi inside the building. The next day, *Jornal dos Sports* published a photo of Valtinho, Romário and Kaiser taken outside the hotel; just three wealthy footballers fighting the cause for their less fortunate colleagues.

Kaiser had the picture of himself, Valtinho and Romário laminated and carried it around in his wallet. A few months later, he was at a salad bar in Leblon. 'I vividly remember where we were,' says Valtinho, 'because he was in a phase of eating only salad for his weird bodybuilding diet.' Valtinho was talking when Kaiser suddenly got up and walked off. Valtinho turned around to see him chatting to a woman.

'Who is the best looking of us three?'

'Hang on, isn't that Romário? What are you doing in a picture with Romário?'

'Well ... '

Valtinho shakes his head as he tells the story. 'It was another girl he managed to charm with his peculiar methods. I think he still has that photo.'

It's not the only thing he has kept. Kaiser has a collection of photographs, videos, newspaper articles, even little team sheet boxes that include the name Henrique. You never know when you might need to do a bit of marketing.

\*\*\*

Fluminense struggled at the start of the 1995 Campeonato Carioca, and many thought Renato Gaúcho was finished: he was thirty-two years old, struggling with injury and had just had a poor spell at Atlético Mineiro. 'Botafogo and Flamengo were doing really well,' says Renato. 'Túlio and Romário were scoring loads and everyone was asking: "Who will be the King of Rio?" And even though we were nine points behind, I said, "I'll be the King of Rio. Fluminense will go all the way." Everyone said I was crazy.'

Túlio's Botafogo finished third, behind Flamengo and Fluminense, although they had the considerable consolation of becoming champions of Brazil. At the time, though, it was probably more prestigious to be champion of Rio than of Brazil, and the last match of the Campeonato Carioca, played in front of a crowd of 109,000, was a classic that went straight into folklore.

The league table was such that Fluminense needed to beat Flamengo, who in turn only needed a draw. It was also Fla–Flu, the most celebrated derby in Rio football; the aristocrats against the team of the people.

Renato and Leonardo put Fluminense 2-0 up at half-time. Then Romário and Fabinho – not to be confused with Kaiser's former Ajaccio colleague – made it 2-2. With three minutes to go, Ailton dribbled into the area and hit a shot towards goal that deflected in off Renato's chest. It went down in legend as Renato's 'belly goal'. Some still say it was Ailton's goal, or that Renato scored with his hand, though replays suggest he instinctively twisted his body to chest it over the line.

The semantic argument didn't change the fact that Renato's Fluminense were the champions of Rio, and it certainly didn't stop him letting everyone know who the King of Rio was. He still does so more than twenty years later. 'I didn't score in many games against the smaller teams,' says Renato, 'but in all the big games at the Maracanã, mainly against Flamengo, I scored. When it comes to the big games, the big players turn up.'

Renato went to bed at 7 a.m. the next day, after a hard night's coronation, and was soon woken for a photoshoot in which the press encouraged him to dress up in full costume with a sceptre and crown. He looked utterly, brilliantly ridiculous. 'My only regret,' he says, 'is that I didn't get Kaiser to do the photos.'

There are some who think that would have been appropriate. 'Romário and Renato were just squabbling while the real king of Rio was Kaiser,' says Alexandre Torres. 'They wanted to usurp the place of a guy that was impossible to dethrone.'

\*\*\*

The fallout from Flamengo's defeat included an inevitable change of coach. The artistic differences between Romário and the coach Vanderlei Luxemburgo became irreconcilable and Luxemburgo was sacked. His replacement, Edinho, lasted a couple of months. As speculation mounted over who would be next in line, the journalist Washington Rodrigues received a call from the Flamengo chairman Kleber Leite, who invited him round to discuss who should get the job. Rodrigues suggested Tele Santana. Leite disagreed, and pointed to an upturned plate, underneath which was the name of the man they wanted to manage Flamengo: Washington Rodrigues.

'This is a joke,' he said.

'No. You're a tough guy and it's a really tricky situation."

By the time Rodrigues agreed to take the job it was 5 a.m. and his wife was questioning his sanity, especially as his relationship with the team's best player, Romário, was less than perfect. 'I arrived there having fought with him but he was so kind and he was always trying to help. The same with Edmundo. He turns into an animal on the pitch but off the field he's so nice. I thought the world of both of them. I wasn't too bad as a coach. I'm the only Flamengo coach not to be fired, that's on my CV. But those two played a huge part.'

\*\*\*

When Kaiser's friend and former Ajaccio team-mate Alexandre Couto joined America de Três Rios, a lower-league club, Kaiser went with him. He even put his boots on, and was doing his usual skit of avoiding the ball during training when Alexandre decided to play a prank. Alexandre pointed to the far side of the field and smashed a disguised pass in the other direction, straight to the feet of Kaiser. As the America de Três Rios captain came to close Kaiser down, Alexandre and others shouted, 'Man on!' Kaiser, flustered by the hot potato at his feet, panicked and flicked it up in the air. As he did so the captain slid in, missed the ball completely and ended up face down in the dirt. It looked as if Kaiser had duped him with a sublime piece of skill.

In reality it was the football equivalent of a stopped clock telling the right time at least twice a day. It was all too emotional for Kaiser, who immediately fell over screaming that he had injured his leg. 'He flicked it over the guy through complete fluke,' laughs Alexandre Couto. 'The guy almost snapped him in half. Then he tried to hunt Kaiser down because everybody was taking the piss out of him.'

When he returned from injury, Kaiser decided to get involved with some physical training. The kit man, prompted by Alexandre, gave Kaiser shorts that were a size large – except unbeknownst to Kaiser they were a kid's size large. Kaiser complained but was told they were the only shorts they had.

'Those shorts were like Lycra,' says Alexandre. 'Everybody was laughing at him, saying, "What's that, mate? Are you going to do some ballet?" It was a complete mess.'

Kaiser squeaked and moaned his way round a couple of laps of the pitch before he heard a rip and took himself for an early bath. He didn't return the next day.

\*\*\*

Even though Kaiser was thirty-three, approaching retirement age for many footballers, his media profile continued to grow. In another newspaper feature, it was reported that Kaiser was considering offers from Olympiacos and Panathinaikos in Greece. It also gave a tantalising glimpse of a new, bohemian side. The article was accompanied by a picture of Kaiser with his head forward, a look of solemn profundity on his face, and two crystal earrings in his hand.

'Carlos Kaizer [sic] distances himself from the footballer stereotype. He doesn't use slang or soundbites and he is articulate about many issues other than football. Esoteric, Kaizer believes in the power of crystals and even his look is influenced by this philosophy. He has an earring in both ears ("to draw energy") and long hair: "I wear my hair long so people can't touch my head. It's one of the vital parts of our body and not everybody should be able to touch it. To prevent this from happening, I tell people that I don't want my hair messed up."'

\*\*\*

The highlight of the 1997 Campeonato Carioca final between Botafogo and Vasco da Gama was not a goal, a red card; not even a corner. It occurred when a loose ball drifted out to the right wing. Edmundo kept it in play and then, as the Botafogo defender Gonçalves came towards him, demonstratively leaned forward and placed both hands on his thighs. Gonçalves, knowing Edmundo's maverick nature, stepped cautiously towards the ball, like a bomb-disposal expert approaching a suspect package. As he did so, Edmundo, still with his hands on his thighs, started wiggling his backside from side to side. Then he exploded away from Gonçalves before being tackled by another Botafogo player. Edmundo's showboating almost led to a punch-up on the field. It became known as the 'danca da bundinha' – or, as Gonçalves puts it in pidgin English twenty years later, the 'shake-yo-ass dance'.

It's not hard to guess what happened next. Botafogo won the Campeonato Carioca after a 1-0 victory in the second leg a few days later, and Gonçalves celebrated by doing the Edmundo dance in front of the opposing Vasco fans. It was a night for memorable celebrations. The goalscorer Dimba got down on all fours and started eating the Maracanã grass.

Edmundo was in the headlines again during that summer's Copa América in Bolivia, most notably when he chinned a Bolivian defender. His career never quite took off – at international level he had to compete with Ronaldo, Romário, Bebeto and others, and a spell at Fiorentina turned sour when, with the club fighting to win Serie A for the first time in thirty years, he went AWOL so that he could visit Rio carnival.

'I think Edmundo missed the chance to become one of the best players in the world,' says Washington Rodrigues. 'He has exceptional dedication. He transformed into a beast when he played football. But he didn't manage to moderate that so there was a lot of friction and he ended up having bust-ups with loads of people. He was very short-tempered with the press and even with his own directors. When I managed him I got to know his story really well. I found out that he blames life. He blames his childhood when he had to sleep on the floor of a grand-pa's barber shop. He blames being abandoned. He blames people for not valuing him when he was younger. So he has a kind of chip on his shoulder where he wants to show himself to be something he's not. And because of all that he missed out on signing big contracts and playing for Barcelona or Real Madrid.'

It would be reasonable to suggest Edmundo divides opinion. 'He was totally out of his mind,' says the journal-ist Renato Maurício Prado. 'He still is. I love not being at Fox since they hired him. Don't even think about work-ing with him. Edmundo's a nutcase, who's now posing as a pundit. But in football terms he was a great player, without a doubt.'

***

Renato Mendes Mota was keen to catch up with Kaiser. He had barely seen his old friend since moving to Manaus to become a lawyer but made sure to meet up every time he was back in Rio. This time they planned to meet for dinner at a Japanese restaurant in Alto Tijuca. Mota was tight for time and called Kaiser to see if he could squash two catch-ups into one.

'Kaiser, do you mind if we have dinner with my friend Carlinhos as well tomorrow? I really want to see him and I need to fly back straight after.'

'Carlinhos? Is he the one who looks like Valdir Espinosa?'

'The Botafogo coach Valdir Espinosa?'

'Yeah.'

'I hadn't thought about it but I suppose he does now you mention it.'

'Great, bring him along. I've got a plan.'

Kaiser arrived the following day along with a girl he was keen to impress. Renato Mota was to be his cousin, a lawyer who was overseeing a potential transfer. Mota's friend, who had the look of somebody in authority, was an agent who had been flown over to discuss a possible move to Germany or Japan.

Kaiser could not have played his role better if he believed it was all true.

'So how many millions of dollars are they talking about?'

'Japan are offering more: around $400,000 a season. Bayern Munich are offering less but you have to decide which is best.'

'It's harder for Brazilian players to adapt in Asia. But there's a chance to learn a new culture. I know that isn't important for most footballers but it is for me. I've always been interested in Japan: the serenity, discipline and respect they have in their culture really appeals to a Buddhist like me.'

Kaiser instructed his agent to go ahead with the move to Japan, and went off into the night with a girl who now thought he was a football superstar.

\*\*\*

With the 1998 World Cup approaching, Brazil were looking formidable. They were beginning to demonstrate an attacking flair worthy of the 1980s team, particularly with the exhilarating strike partnership of Ronaldo and Romário ('RoRo', as it became known). The world did not get to see RoRo in France. Romário suffered a muscular injury and was eventually omitted from the World Cup squad by Mário Zagallo. It was a bitter blow, and he was in tears at a press conference. He was then sued by both Zagallo and Zico, his No. 2, after putting unflattering caricatures of them on the toilet doors of his bar, Café de Gol.

It is one of the bigger what-ifs in football history: two decades on, the thought of Romário and peak Ronaldo together in France still rouses the hairs on the back of the neck. In the short time they were together they left defenders at their wits' end, their brains melting with the demands of concentrating against them for ninety minutes. England's Gary Neville, who played in the centre of defence against Brazil during Le Tournoi in 1997, recalled Ronaldo and Romário laughing their heads off at a joke while play was going on at the other end and England's defenders were gulping oxygen.

Ronaldo, a non-playing member of the 1994 World Cup-winning squad, had emerged as the most exciting player in the world. He was possibly the greatest young footballer of all time, an awesome blend of skill, speed and power. He was faster with the ball than most people were without it. 'Ronaldo could start from the halfway line and the whole stadium would ignite,' said Sir Bobby Robson, his manager at Barcelona. 'A current would course through the stands.'

That was because Ronaldo played like a winger – but he did so in the centre of the pitch, which made him infinitely more dangerous. He played like every attack had a ten-second deadline and was like a bulldozer that could go at 90mph.

That Barcelona team is seen as one of the great coaching seminars, with Pep Guardiola, Luis Enrique and Laurent Blanc on the pitch and José Mourinho on the bench. Ronaldo did not bother with all that theory. At his best he was the antonym of tiki-taka: he just ran through everything and scored a goal.

Kaiser is occasionally compared to Ronaldo – and this time he's not the one making the comparison. 'Brazil is actually a privileged country,' says the Ajaccio attacker Fabinho. 'We have two phenomena. One on the pitch called Ronaldo, a No. 9 who did unbelievable things. And off the pitch, Carlos Kaiser, the phenomenon who did things nobody else in the world could do.'

\*\*\*

When Romário was left out, Bebeto came into the starting XI, with Edmundo on the bench. They also had the emerging Rivaldo, the stepover-loving Denilson – the world's most expensive player, who had joined Real Betis from São Paulo for £21.5 million – and Leonardo.

The Nike advert for the 1998 World Cup is one of football's famous promos, with the players running through an airport demonstrating all kinds of impossible ball skills. Not even Kaiser could gate-crash that one.

Brazil strutted through the tournament, with Ronaldo close to unstoppable at times. They lost their final group game, a dead rubber against Norway, and lived on the edge defensively, but they always seemed to have enough attacking talent to get them out of trouble – in the knockout stages they beat Chile 4-1, Denmark 3-2 and Holland on penalties in the semi-finals after an immense 1-1 draw.

The holders France had struggled to reach the final, heavily dependent on their peerless defence both for clean sheets and goals. Brazil were favourites for the final. We all know what happened next. Well, partially. Ronaldo was taken to hospital and excluded from the XI before being reinstated, and a distracted Brazil were hammered 3-0 by France. Bixente Lizarazu, the France left-back, called it their easiest game of a tournament in which they played South Africa and Saudi Arabia.

The official and most credible story is that Ronaldo had a convulsion on the afternoon of the game, something that had never happened before or since; he was unconscious for a few minutes before being taken to hospital, where he felt normal and decided to go to the ground. After a heated dressing-room argument, Zagallo put him back in the team. There were strong suggestions that Nike's influence had crossed the line, and that they demanded Ronaldo be included. The case even went to court, though that proved to be a waste of everyone's time. We will probably never know the full truth.

# CHAPTER 28

# THE FORMER FOOTBALLER

Búzios, the idyllic resort in the south-east of Rio de Janeiro, is Kaiser's favourite place on earth. 'A beautiful place for beautiful people,' he says, matter-of-factly including himself in such company. Some of the greatest parties of Kaiser's life were in Búzios – particularly around Christmas and New Year, when the domestic footballers were on their break and a number of foreign-based players also returned home.

'Nightlife in Búzios starts at 1 a.m. and ends at midday,' says Kaiser. 'If you're famous, people leave you in peace. Nobody mobs you like in Rio de Janeiro. I used to come here when I was on my Christmas break from Ajaccio.'

The players spent the daytime lazing at the beach, playing footvolley, drinking cold beer and chatting to local admirers. One day Kaiser went off on his own, jogging up and down the main beach wearing only a cap, sunglasses and exquisitely tight orange shorts. Nobody knew what he was up to – until the early hours of the following morning, when they were talking to a group of women.

'Did I see you jogging along the beach today? You had orange shorts on?'

'Yeah, I'm on my winter break from Real Madrid – I need to keep in shape as we have some really important fixtures in January. Have you ever been to Madrid, by the way?'

Kaiser came to Búzios with some of the superstars of Brazilian football: Renato Gaúcho, Gonçalves, Gaúcho, Carlos Alberto Torres, Branco, Tato and the rest. A match against a Búzios XI became an annual tradition. 'It was the biggest game of the year for them,' says Kaiser. 'They'd be cooped up and we'd be going out to a nightclub until midday when the game was at 2 p.m. Imagine if we'd lost the game. We had over fifty women watching the game against the best in Búzios. You'd think we'd lose a game like that?'

The agent Frankie Henouda owned the elite Le Club, the trendiest nightclub in Búzios, and Kaiser became the manager. Each night he strutted around flaunting his status, deciding who could and could not enter the club. 'Le Club was a place of fun and happiness, flirting, hooking up, sex,' says Kaiser. 'There was a strategic exit and a private area where they did their sexual business. All the celebrities did that rather than go back to wherever they were staying. It was the most natural thing in the world. Nowadays the cool nightclub is Privilégio. The ones who ran the show back then were me, Renato and Gaúcho. Now Romário rules the roost because Privilégio is the main nightclub in Juiz de Fora and he's a king there. In the kingdom of the blind, the one-eyed man is king.'

Renato Gaúcho also had a spectacular holiday home in Búzios, where he would host New Year's Eve parties. Each year Renato had a special T-shirt printed, which doubled up as a stamp that allowed entry. Kaiser diligently went round getting rid of the gatecrashers and imposters.

\*\*\*

Renato Mendes Mota was woken by the sound of somebody thumping an adjoining wall. It was 5 a.m. and he was staying in a rented villa in Búzios with a group of friends including Kaiser. It soon became apparent that the thumping was an accompaniment to Kaiser having sex, and that he had woken everyone else up as well. The next day, one of the group announced he was going home because he had barely slept a wink. 'No worries,' said Kaiser. 'But could you leave your blender? I need to make my protein shakes and you promised I could use it all week.'

\*\*\*

If Búzios was Kaiser's favourite place to visit, then the Rio Sul shopping mall was still his day-to-day residence. One afternoon in 2001, while recovering from an eye operation that left him struggling to see much beyond the end of his nose, he was chatting with Valtinho and some other players. It was not just any old afternoon: there was a scheduled appearance by Ivete Sangalo, a twenty-nine-year-old pop singer whose debut solo album had recently gone platinum. Kaiser, hearing all the noise, assumed the commotion was because of all the footballers in the mall.

He started chatting to Sangalo, oblivious to who she was. For the next ten minutes, Kaiser explained to one of Brazil's biggest superstars that it was a nightmare being famous. When you played for Manchester United, he said, it was hard to get much peace and quiet.

He may not have been able to see but Kaiser could still talk, and he somehow charmed Sangalo enough that she agreed to go on a date. He took her to Toro, where he had one of his sponsorships, and was still unaware that he was in the company of one of the most famous people in Brazil. Kaiser talked so much at Rio Sul that he had not even asked her what she did for a living. When they were in Toro, Kaiser, noticing that everyone was staring at their table, repeatedly apologised for the lack of privacy. 'This,' he said, 'is what I have to put up with every day.' There was no second date.

Most of Kaiser's short-term relationships ended amicably enough. There were a couple of notable exceptions. Once he dated two sisters simultaneously, using money from one to buy presents for the other. It lasted a few months before unravelling. 'They both went to his apartment to have a go at him,' says Renato Mendes Mota. 'It was complete chaos.'

In 2001, Kaiser was dating a woman who regularly chauffeured him around Rio and paid for dinner. When Kaiser broke up with her, she went to the police and complained that he was a 171. Nothing came of that, so the woman cast a black magic spell on him instead. Kaiser brusquely informed her that the aforementioned Pai Santana, one of Rio's most famous black magic priests, had already tried and failed to do that at Vasco da Gama.

\*\*\*

Back in the real world of football, a career-threatening knee injury kept Ronaldo out for most of the four years between the 1998 and 2002 World Cups. He returned just before the tournament in Japan and Korea, which Brazil won in style. They were easily the best team in a poor competition, with Ronaldo finding redemption by scoring both goals in a 2-0 win over Germany in the final. He scored eight goals in the tournament, the most in a single World Cup since 1970, and formed a devastating attack with Rivaldo and Ronaldinho. After that, however, the fantasy again drained out of Brazilian football. They were knocked out in the quarter-finals in 2006 and 2010, and then there was 2014.

Brazil's 7-1 defeat to Germany in the semi-final of that World Cup might be the most staggering result in the history of football. It was particularly twisted that, after twenty-five years of focusing largely on a more defensive game, Brazil then haemorrhaged goals during their own World Cup semi-final. It was as if somebody up there was punishing them for messing with the natural order.

Brazil still produce players of attacking genius like Neymar and Roberto Firmino, but there aren't so many to go around. And in a post-Dunga world, Brazil are arguably best known for producing defensive midfielders. Think of any elite European club, and the likelihood is they will have had a Brazilian holding player in the last decade.

There is an eternal debate about the balance between skill and strength. 'Youth coaching in Brazil focuses too much on athleticism and gym work,' says Alexandre Couto. He highlights Hulk, the huge forward who played in the 2014 World Cup. 'What the fuck is Hulk? He's a UFC fighter.'

It's a recurring theme. 'In the 1980s Maradona said something that's stuck with me,' says Washington Rodrigues. 'He said, "You can find a great player under every rock in Brazil." Nowadays when you lift up a rock there are just bugs. There isn't the same kind of regeneration. All this modernity and urbanisation has had an impact. When I was a young boy in Rio there were at least twelve pitches near my house. Great players are made on the earth and the sand, playing barefoot. You don't have that anymore. We produce human machines that can play consistently well for ninety minutes. Skill is a bonus. A lot of kids these days don't even bother. They are great video-game players but on the pitch they're useless.'

The reaction to the Germany humiliation, and the appointment of Tite as coach, helped Brazil rediscover some of their football identity. 'It will never be as free, light and happy as it was because football has changed,' says Martha Esteves, 'but I think it's coming back with people like Neymar.'

Neymar is the only Brazilian to come anywhere near winning the Ballon d'Or in the last decade, when he finished third in 2015. From 1997 to 2007 the award went to a Brazilian player on five occasions: Ronaldo twice, Rivaldo, Ronaldinho and Kaká. Since then, nothing.

When Neymar moved to Paris-Saint Germain in 2017, his wages rose to €37 million per year. 'Football is big business these days,' says Edgar Pereira. 'It's much more professional. And it was 7-1 to Germany.'

\*\*\*

As his football career wound down, Kaiser started to pursue an alternative profession. He became a fitness trainer and found he was actually good at it. With that and his unofficial work as a promoter, he was forced to come to a sad decision. In July 2003, on his fortieth birthday, Kaiser phoned a couple of local newspapers to announce his retirement. The news didn't quite stop the press. As he hung up his unblemished boots, Kaiser reflected on a career with so many stories, so many highs and lows, and a perfect record: 0 games, 0 goals. 'Footballers die twice,' he says. 'When we stop playing and then when we actually die. I've lost one life already.'

His second life gathered momentum a year later when the journalist Renato Maurício Prado wrote about him in the newspaper *O Globo*. Prado told the story of how Kaiser hoodwinked Castor de Andrade by fighting with the fans at Bangu, and how he had built a career as a footballer without kicking a ball.

'A good journalist is a storyteller,' says Prado. 'And if they know how to make it clear that the story is kind of a myth, that's fine. Kaiser's story is a mythical story, and that's why I put it in the column. We, the press, will fall for anything people tell us. Do you believe that Túlio Maravilha scored a thousand goals? It's one of the biggest lies in world football and we believed it. We're always looking for a big story. Kaiser must have played with Túlio Maravilha. Half of Túlio's thousand goals probably came from assists by Kaiser.

'If you look at the funny side of it, Kaiser's story is amazing. He did a lot better than he should have done in life, thanks to fraud. He's a legendary character in football. I don't think he's done anything evil. I wouldn't arrest Kaiser. I wouldn't sentence Kaiser. On the contrary. I think he's become a source of great amusement.'

It's hard to imagine Kaiser's story happening again. Globalisation, technology, professionalism and a greater circulation of information would make it impossible for somebody to talk their way into so many clubs. 'He impersonated a footballer for over twenty years,' says Renato Gaúcho. 'Nobody will ever come close to him. They wouldn't have the slightest chance. Our Kaiser always has and always will be unique. He is the greatest footballer never to play football.'

He was also the greatest lover never to fall in love. And then something extraordinary happened.

# CHAPTER 29

# THE HUSBAND

Kaiser always boasted that no woman could penetrate his heart. But when he met Marcella Mendes, a former ballerina and model, at his gym, he felt something he didn't understand. It was mutual. 'She was like an obsession,' says Kaiser. 'We were both in a relationship but she dropped everything and so did I.'

They had only been together a few months when Kaiser asked Marcella to marry him. He had never been so sure of anything in his life. When she said yes, the two could not wait and went straight to a registry office. 'She was beautiful, hot, wonderful, coveted by many men,' says Renato Gaúcho. 'And who married her? Carlos Kaiser. Explain that to me. He was broke and he married Marcella. It's his charisma.'

Kaiser became a diffcrent person; not really Kaiser at all. He disappeared from the old social circles and spent the next few years hosting dinner parties at the marital flat in Leme, where he lived next door to Romário. One of the regular visitors was Valtinho, Kaiser's friend from America, and his wife. 'Marcella was delicate, elegant, intelligent and polite,' says Valtinho. 'She was a really strong person and a really good influence on Kaiser.'

Marcella was bright and effervescent; a gentle soul who made Kaiser see the world through different eyes. He started to enjoy simple pleasures like cooking, watching films and telling the truth. He spent a lot more time at the gym and started a sports science course.

'She organised his life and gave him a feeling of family he'd never really had,' says Valtinho. 'They had a lovely apartment in Leme. And then all of a sudden she died.'

Marcella died of brain ischemia, a condition in which there is insufficient blood flow to the brain. It had a devastating impact on Kaiser: Valtinho uses the phrase 'perdeu chão', which literally means to lose the floor beneath you.

'We didn't even get to say goodbye,' says Kaiser. 'That was the biggest shock of my life, and the biggest loss. Nothing will ever come close. I'd do anything to have her back. If happiness exists, I was happy when I was with her. I forgot my past.'

'I never cheated on my wife. Seriously, never. I wouldn't have cheated on her for a fivesome. On the day we got married she said, "I'm afraid of losing you, of you leaving me." I was never going to leave that woman. I wanted to grow old with her.'

Whether through fatalism, desperation or fear, Kaiser slowly returned to his old ways. Except now he was a man in his forties, with all the inherent physical and psychological limitations, and one who was nowhere near getting over the death of his wife. 'I internalised all the grief,' he says. 'My life went properly off the rails. I lost all sense of right and wrong.'

The re-emergence of Kaiser came as a surprise to many of his old friends, who had lost touch with him. 'He vanished for maybe five or six years,' says Dror Niv. 'He just disappeared. When he returned he was down and out. He didn't have hot women, he had no car, he had nobody to pay his bills. It was a different story. In the first period he was kind of a gigolo. He would meet properly beautiful women from middle-class and upper-class families. They would drive him around and pay the bill. Then as time went by the girls were still pretty but they were from more modest neighbourhoods. And then came those really toned, muscular women who were old. Really old.'

# CHAPTER 30

# THE FITNESS TRAINER

It was a Sunday night and Kaiser had invited his friend Leri Da Rosa to come out with him. He was planning to go to Nuth, a posh nightclub in Barra, where he was friends with the owner. 'There's women everywhere,' said Kaiser. 'You won't have to worry about anything as it's all on my tab and I know everybody there.'

When they arrived, they found a queue that seemed to go on forever. Kaiser marched straight past the queue as usual and led Leri round the back of the club. He assumed they were heading to the VIP entrance. 'Kaiser opened a door and walked through,' says Da Rosa. 'I followed him and the first thing I saw was a deep-fat fryer. We were in the kitchen! It was absolutely roasting in there. Once we finally got into the club I realised that he'd just snuck in like a rat. I was so embarrassed. I said to him "Fucking hell, Kaiser, I work. I can just go to the front and pay the entrance fee, I don't need this shit!"'

Kaiser – and his friends – were realising the hard way that old footballers don't always get on the VIP list. Being a fitness trainer had nothing like the same glamour, even if Kaiser was genuinely good at it. He worked hard to publicise himself at every opportunity, and even pushed for the creation of new categories like 'Wellness' just so that his pupils could win competitions.

He still found ways to get himself in the papers. It was headline news when, in April 2008, Romário's Ferrari was written off after a crash in Icarai. He had lent the car to a friend while at a party. The next day, when Romário turned up to have his car towed, he found Kaiser waiting for him. Kaiser asked if he could do anything to help. An already exasperated Romário said no. It didn't matter – the paparazzi had taken pictures of the two together, some of which appeared in the following day's newspapers.

\*\*\*

Kaiser's life took another turn in 2011, when Marco Tioco, who had been a press officer at Botafogo in the 1990s, suggested he sell his story. 'I don't think he realised how interesting his story was,' says Tioco. 'He was so deeply entrenched that he only started to understand what he was doing, and what he represented, after he'd stopped. He started to understand that he was a character in a funny story. The least I could do was help him with press connections.'

It was time for Kaiser to tell the truth, the occasional truth and something resembling the truth. He was pitched as the Forrest Gump of football, and Tioco arranged an exclusive interview on *Esporte Espetacular*, a regular show on Globo TV. Kaiser walked around Rio telling his story to the presenter Renato Ribeiro. At the end Kaiser looked straight to camera, took off his sunglasses and did a bit of marketing: 'Whoever needs a personal trainer, just look for me, Carlos Henrique Kaiser. I'm better than the football player – that's a guarantee.'

That was small beer compared to Kaiser's next appearance a month later. *The Jô Soares Show* was the biggest chat show in South America, a Brazilian version of *David Letterman* that was often the most watched programme in Brazil.

'Carlos Kaiser on *Jô Soares*? I don't believe that,' says Washington Rodrigues. 'I'll believe it when I see it. And even then I won't believe it. That show is an institution in Brazilian TV. As well as being a cultured and intelligent person, Jo is a polymath because he's a theatre director, a humourist and a wonderful interviewer.'

Soares's range of talents is such that he was once described as 'the Renaissance man of Brazilian popular culture'. He would often interview guests in other languages and act as his own translator. All the greats of Brazilian football have been on the show: Pelé, Ronaldo, Neymar, Romário, Zico. And Carlos Kaiser.

He blagged his way onto the show, offering to talk about his career as a fake footballer. But whenever Soares asked a question about football, Kaiser answered one about his current career. He was using the biggest talk show in the country to advertise his services as a fitness trainer.

Before anyone had chance to say, 'This isn't quite what we envisaged when we invited you on', Kaiser asked if he could call one of his students from the crowd to sit next to him because 'she makes me feel more comfortable on TV'.

Soon she was the star of the show, performing a demonstration of her physique – and therefore Kaiser's teaching – that bore more than a little resemblance to an old-fashioned striptease. Within seconds she was strutting round the stage wearing only a sports bikini and high heels.

Inevitably, it was a set-up. She wasn't a student of Kaiser's at all, just a beautiful and buff woman called Fabiola who he had approached in the street with the chance of a lifetime. Fabiola was the talk of *The Jô Soares Show*, and over the next few weeks Kaiser had hundreds of new applications.

\*\*\*

Having spent a few years in the doldrums, Kaiser had a taste for fame again. In December 2011, the hulking striker Adriano, whose career and life had gone downhill since a successful spell in Italy with Internazionale, was involved in a notorious incident in Barra. He was reported to have accidentally shot a woman in the hand when they were in his car, though a few days later she said she pulled the trigger.

Another woman, who was also in the car at the time, was widely photographed when she arrived at the police station the following day. Kaiser found out she was a body-builder named Andrea Ximenez – and that she was the cousin of the sushi chef who worked at Dror Niv's I Piatti restaurant. 'He moved heaven and earth until he got her number,' says Niv. Kaiser, who had been developing a nice sideline in selling supplements for bodybuilders, soon became Ximenez's boyfriend and her personal trainer.

Soon after, Kaiser booked a table at I Piatti for him, his new love and a few close friends. At the end, he got down on one knee and proposed. She accepted and everybody went home high on the joys of love. Except the happy couple: Niv saw them part ways about fifty yards from the restaurant. 'She got in one taxi and he got in another,' he says. 'It was a scam. It was all for some supplement sponsor.'

\*\*\*

In 2012, Kaiser was less than impressed to see that one of his students, a transsexual named Paloma, had told a newspaper they were dating. The article was accompanied by a picture of Kaiser and Paloma leaning in for a smooch. 'She was a funk dancer,' he says. 'She was only performing once a month before saying she was involved with me. Then she suddenly started doing ten shows a week. Profiting from the fact she'd been with a footballer. If the shoe was on the other foot I'd have said nothing. But people often use footballers. What can you do?"

If there's one thing Kaiser hates, it's hangers-on.

# CHAPTER 31

# THE FANTASY FOOTBALLER

Kaiser's spell at Ajaccio defined his career. It gave him stories – 'when the pitch is flooded I shoot from behind the goal' – that were lapped up in dressing rooms, while the status of being somebody who played in France helped open doors all over Rio.

And none of it actually happened.

That, at least, is the truth according to Fabinho, the attacker who was supposed to have brought Kaiser to the club in 1987. He says Kaiser has never set foot in Corsica, never mind been on the books of Ajaccio; that Kaiser borrowed memorabilia and manipulated it to make himself seem like an exotic, foreign-based footballer. Or, to put it another way, that he stole Fabinho's identity.

'It helped him that Ajaccio was so far away because it was impossible for people to research a second division team in France,' he says. 'I gave him shirts from Ajaccio and other clubs in the French league.'

He also gave him a blank Ajaccio ID card, which became Kaiser's most cherished possession. 'He said to me, "This is the best Christmas present I'll ever receive!"' Kaiser borrowed Fabinho's card and produced a perfect replica, even down to the club emblem. 'I can't believe he could get the card exactly the same. The stamp was perfect.'

Kaiser's Ajaccio ID became a universal key card. He had it laminated and used it to get in everywhere from restaurants and nightclubs – 'I'm on holiday in Rio, I just want to have a look around' – to the Maracanã. It also ensured free rooms, free meals and other gratuities. 'That card was a status symbol for him,' says Fabinho. 'It was like an official document which even helped him get onto loads of TV shows. This created the idea that Kaiser was in France, Argentina, Mexico and many other places, when the only time he left Rio was to go to El Paso.'

It gives a whole new meaning to fantasy football.

\*\*\*

Alexandre Couto, who also played for Ajaccio, originally said he was there with Kaiser. When he was interviewed a second time, having spoken to Fabinho, he told a different story. 'Kaiser never played for Ajaccio,' he says. 'I love Kaiser to bits and we've always done everything to indulge his fantasy, because these football stories are his daily bread. But lying on behalf of him has become uncomfortable. When Fabinho told me he had spoken the truth I decided to do the same. I really love Kaiser, but I have to be fair.'

Like Fabinho, Alexandre gave Kaiser lots of Ajaccio paraphernalia; everything from pristine match shirts to rosettes. 'I don't have any Ajaccio memorabilia left,' he says. 'It's all in Kaiser's house!'

Just as crucially, they gave him an encyclopaedia's worth of detail about the experience of being an Ajaccio player. Kaiser asked about everything, from the weather to the fashion to the name of the club captain to whether they had love motels.

'He would ask me what life was like in Corsica, what the diet was like,' says Fabinho. 'He made up all that stuff about the nights out and Mancini having mafia connections. None of that is true. He created a film for himself.'

The story was told in a hodgepodge of Portuguese and French. 'He learned a few French phrases from me: "*Comme ci, comme ça*", "*Parlez-vous français*", "*Je t'aime*". That was the phrase he'd use with the ladies. If you had a conversation with him, I doubt he'd be able to put a full sentence together.'

***

There is a collection of pictures, taken in the late 1980s, of Kaiser at the Ajaccio training ground. They were used in various newspaper profiles and features throughout Kaiser's career. The camera may never lie, but sometimes the caption does. 'That's actually Clube dos Macacos in south Rio,' says Fabinho. 'It's an exclusive sports club so only a few people would recognise that the photos were taken there. He must have asked the person taking the photo not to include the whole pitch, just a small part.'

A visit to Clube dos Macacos with Fabinho confirmed the similarities between Kaiser's photos, taken thirty years ago, and the club today. The backdrop of palm trees is identical.

Fabinho also recognised Kaiser's attire. 'That's a training top that I'd brought from Ajaccio,' he says, looking at one picture. Another has Kaiser in full match kit. 'This is the Ajaccio match shirt from the 1986–7 season. It was as if I'd brought him a piece of treasure. This stuff was pure gold for him because with that he could turn himself into a professional player. Somebody who's not very familiar with football might think he was playing there. But it looks kind of weird because at training you usually have loads of players around. And you would never wear the match shirt during training.'

Another picture has Kaiser with his right hand in the air, his index finger pointing impatiently. 'Man, there's one that is really funny,' says Fabinho. 'Him calling for the ball. "Pass the fucking ball!" He had all the little tricks and mannerisms of a professional player. He liked to crouch down and look around like a player. He would pull his shorts up a bit to show off his legs. The shorts were really tight in the eighties. It was really suggestive and that was his intention. He took the photos exactly so women could see that he was really playing for a French team.

'If he was studying for a degree, he would have nailed the theory side of being a footballer. He would even kick with the outside of the foot because that's how all the classy players did it. But anybody in the industry would quickly notice that it was fake.'

When Kaiser originally showed Alexandre the photos, the response did not go down well.

'Oh great, that's in Clube dos Macacos.'

'You're a dick.'

'Kaiser, do you want to teach me about where all the pitches are in Rio?'

The irritation soon passed, especially as Kaiser had what he wanted. To all intents and purposes he was an Ajaccio player, which increased his profile tenfold. 'Listen, I can guarantee you that he benefited a lot more than I did from having played in Corsica, because I didn't get onto the programmes he did in Rio or go to the places he went,' says Fabinho. 'He went on *Mesa Redonda*. And he gave one of the most famous commentators in Brazil an Ajaccio shirt as a present.'

Being at Ajaccio also gave him an exotic CV when he wanted to approach a new club or a new woman. 'He would tell all sorts of stories,' says Fabinho. 'You have Ali Baba and 1001 Nights. This was Kaiser and 1001 Nights. He told every kind of story imaginable, which the ladies would believe, about his goalscoring and nights out in Corsica. Football was a bridge for him to get everything that he wanted: status and women.'

Kaiser had one last obstacle to overcome if his story was going to work. Why, if he was an Ajaccio player, was he in Rio all the time? That's where the disciplinary measures, for his excessive socialising, and the interminable contract impasse that was mentioned in many newspaper articles – 'I will sell the whole squad but not Charles' – came in. Kaiser sold himself as a misunderstood bad boy, a rogue with a heart of gold.

\*\*\*

There is no resentment from Fabinho that Kaiser stole his story. 'I saw him as completely harmless, so I let him live his fantasy,' he says. 'It was his dream and we encouraged it. We found it so funny. I'm still really fond of him and still speak to him. It doesn't make me angry. He was never a bad person.'

Fabinho was happy to go along with Kaiser's story while it was contained within Rio, but the thought of it spreading to Corsica did not sit comfortably. 'If he wants to keep living his dream, it'll be in his own head. There comes a time when people have to tell the truth. They're really fond of me there and I can't keep telling a huge lie that will find its way back to Europe. In 2011 I was even invited to be the honorary footvolley captain over in Ajaccio. From now on I would rather tell the complete truth. I have my own reputation in a place where I lived and worked for five years, and I can't use my name to promote Carlos Kaiser's lie all around the world. I told him that. He got really pissed off and didn't call me for ages.'

# CHAPTER 32

# THE MAN THEY LEFT BEHIND

Kaiser sits on a pouf in the dimly lit lounge of a modest apartment, jiggling his right knee. His head is angled towards the floor. He is wearing a faded T-shirt, denim shorts, garish red trainers and sunglasses. Behind him is a collage of flyers for takeaways, taxis and gyms. Kaiser is fifty-three years old and this is his life.

It is a few minutes since he heard that Fabinho has spoken about their time at Ajaccio. He does not know Alexandre Couto has also corroborated the story. 'If Fabinho didn't want to talk about it, he should just have said so,' says Kaiser. 'He won't confirm it but there are people who have confirmed it. Alexandre Couto tells the truth. Whatever he says about me, good or bad, it's true.

He's genuine and not two-faced like the other Brazilian. Maybe it's because I got special treatment over there. It's difficult. You can't understand human beings.'

The last few years have not been kind to Kaiser. He has very poor eyesight and a chronic hip problem. When he hears about Fabinho, he has just come out of hospital after being admitted for acid reflux. Many of his peers have died, and the regrets he was able to suppress for so long have muscled their way to the surface. On this day, it is all too much.

He had problems with his eyesight in the early 2000s, when he could not recognise Ivete Sangalo. Things really started to detcriorate in 2013: the week after winning his first trophy as a wellness coach, Kaiser woke up unable to see properly. He has walked straight past a number of his friends, not seeing them in front of him or hearing their hellos amid the chatter of the Rio streets. When he looks at his phone, he holds it barely two inches from his face.

He has had surgery on a swollen cornea in his left eye and also his hip, which is so bad that he walks with a permanent limp. It's a cruel twist that, after so long faking injury, he really does have the body of an old footballer.

Kaiser and many of his friends have noticed that his health started to deteriorate soon after that black magic spell was placed on him in 2001. The journalist Martha Esteves thinks he has *má-fé*, or bad karma. Some of his friends also think he is diabetic. Kaiser is too proud to take the necessary tests to find out.

Most of his medical bills are paid without fanfare by Renato Gaúcho. 'Renato is my father, my friend, my brother, my everything,' says Kaiser. 'I would sacrifice my life for him. I called on the day I lost my eyesight and he interrupted a team talk as Grêmio manager. Usually a guy would get annoyed at that. He was in the middle of his job. He said in the kindest way possible, "Hang in there. When the game finishes, I'll call you." And he did. What can I say about a guy like that? Human beings like that don't exist.'

Kaiser's life of lies has taken a psychological toll as well. A secret is a heavy load, and Kaiser has been carrying ten tonnes on his back for decades. And if you live life to the full, as Kaiser did, there's a danger you'll eventually live it to breaking point. It is notable that there are few mirrors in Kaiser's flat. The one person he struggles to lie to is the man in the mirror.

\*\*\*

Kaiser has no siblings or children able to help him out. He was a father twice when he was younger, but those experiences fill him with regret.

'I didn't see my first son,' he says. 'I wasn't mentally ready to be a father. I met a girl in Mexico City when I was with Puebla. I was only seventeen. But she wanted the child and he was born. His name was Pablo. I never really saw him and I heard later that he died in an earthquake in Mexico City. The tragedy stuck with me.'

Kaiser became a father again in his early twenties during a relationship with a model and actress named Mara Reis. 'I never wanted to have that child. Mara was a great person but it was a difficult relationship. One day she took the car down towards Copacabana and let go of the steering wheel. She said, "If you don't want to have this child all three of us will die." I said, "Fine, let the three of us die then because I don't want that child." But we didn't hit any cars.'

The child was named Carlos Kaiser Alvarenga Leandro, but Kaiser saw very little of his son once he and Mara broke up. 'I made him but I didn't watch him grow up. He admired me from afar. His mum insisted on calling him Carlos Kaiser, so wherever he went the first thing people would ask him is whether he was my son.'

After that, he always wore protection – he says his fear of parenthood was far greater than his fear of HIV. 'As soon as you start talking to me about babies I'll do a runner. It's something that doesn't bring me any pride, having a kid with somebody, I think it's a massive responsibility. I don't deserve to be anyone's father.'

There is a temptation to question everything Kaiser says, but Luiz Maerovitch confirms he did have a son. 'Mara was really eye-catching, a really pretty brunette with long hair down to her waist,' he says. 'Kaiser met her when she was judging a beauty contest. They had a beautiful son. And Kaiser really threw away a family. He didn't invest anything in it. He swapped his family for good and bad friendships, sadly. He preferred to have a nocturnal life rather than a normal one with Mara. I think he was always looking for something more or maybe a chance to show his friends his worth by how many women he could pull or people he could charm.'

Kaiser's friends talk a lot about his missed opportunities, both personal and professional. He was too lost in the moment to think of tomorrow. The upshot is that now, in his fifties, he has very little stability. He continues to do well as a fitness trainer, but in everything else there is a sense of impermanence. He doesn't own a flat, he still has a hole in his pocket, but he no longer has the tools to run Rio de Janeiro. He thought he'd be a footballer forever.

Most of Kaiser's friends regularly encouraged him to put his contacts, brain and instinct for marketing to better use. 'With the mouth he has on him he could have become the most successful agent in the world, because he knows loads of players and had access to all the clubs in Rio,' says Fábio Braz. 'But he always wanted to play the game of getting money by other means. He never wanted an honest job where he had to get up every morning and work hard. He wanted to wake up, go to the beach, hook up with women.'

\*\*\*

A few years ago Kaiser received a call to say his son, who worked for Banco do Brasil in Campos dos Goytacazes, had been killed during a robbery. 'You always think you're going to die before your son. But it's not hard for me to talk about it. There has been a long succession of deaths and losses in my life.'

A number of Kaiser's football friends and acquaint-ances have died in recent years, including Marinho Chagas, Gaúcho, Rocha, Dirceu, Carlos Alberto Torres and Moises. Then there were the deaths of his sons – and the one that took the floor from under him, when his wife Marcella Mendes passed away. 'After she died, I felt so alone so I got together with somebody else,' says Kaiser. 'She died, too. Then another one dies from a heart prob-lem. I thought, "Come on. I'm becoming a gravedigger." Then I wake up one day and I can't see. I don't make any-body answer for that. I don't make God answer for it. I don't ask my friends answer for it. Fuck. Why do I have to suffer so much, man?'

\*\*\*

There are still many people who care deeply about Kaiser – more than he realises – but most have moved onto a different stage of their life, with families and responsibilities. They cannot remember the last time they saw him. 'I got married and left it all behind and didn't hear from him,' says Gonçalves. 'Time went by. Footballers don't always go to the same place so we kind of disbanded.'

It doesn't help that most of the players' wives would, understandably enough, rather their husbands had little to do with him. Yet the affection towards him is enormous. Kaiser is the friend who reminds them of the best days of their lives and they want him to be happy. They know that half of what comes out of his mouth is untrue but they don't care. They don't have to believe him to believe *in* him. 'Kaiser, I don't see you much, because that's life, but you're a brother,' says Valtinho. 'I wish for lots of good things in your life. You're a really special guy and a dear person.'

His health problems are not common knowledge. When Maurício, the Botafogo attacker, was told about Kaiser's struggles, he brushed away tears. 'I hope he achieves his goals, and he has a black brother here,' he says. 'I'm sorry, I didn't know he was having problems.'

Kaiser believes he is suffering a kind of Karmageddon. 'As a Buddhist I believe nothing goes unpunished. In Buddhism we don't believe in Hell. Hell is here, right now. You pay for whatever you do wrong right here. And there is a price for having deceived people, for the mistakes I've made. I believe everything I've done in my life – being inconsiderate, relationships with other people's girlfriends – is coming back. In Buddhism they would say that I lost my vision in order to see the world in a different way. Nowadays I take more care with people's hearts. Life experience makes you more of a man.'

He says he created Kaiser because he was running from the truth of his childhood. Now, at least on the bad days, he struggles with the lies of his adulthood. 'This rogue that everyone imagines is a façade,' he says. 'That's maybe why I've lived other people's lives so much. It was so that I didn't have to stop and think about my life. That Carlos Kaiser who went out to the best places … that guy was built on strong legs. Because Carlos Henrique, he jumped over a lot of hurdles.'

Suddenly Kaiser swings from despair to defiant pride. 'I wasn't born to lose,' he says. 'I really believe in myself. I could have done a lot more right, but I didn't let all the adversity lead me to the dark side. I think I'm a role model. I'm an example that you can play sport and study at the same time. I believe that something good will happen for me. I will build the family I never had.'

\*\*\*

The one constant in Kaiser's life is his work as a wellness and fitness coach. He has his own YouTube show and plugs his work at every opportunity, whether it's approaching strangers on the beach or going on *The Jô Soares Show*. He specialises in bodybuilding, and only coaches women. 'I don't work with meatheads or guys,' he says. 'The rest of the market is all for them. I only work with women who want to become showgirls with a hot body. I've trained thirty-five bodybuilding champions in the last ten years. I'm not just a good wellness trainer, I'm the best. And most of the women I get involved with sexually and emotionally are all from the wellness category.'

Even in his fifties, Kaiser still has a ferocious sexual appetite. There are touches of the old vanity, too. Dror Niv noticed that, as he got older, Kaiser would never take a shower in public or get his hair wet because it exposed a bald patch that he covered by pushing his hair across. He also dyes it jet black.

There is still a spark of mischief, especially when he is telling stories about the stories. 'If a chance to talk about football comes up he'll begin to relive all his past successes,' says Gil. 'And with the mouth he has on him he'll deceive you and get something from you. He's a sweet talker so he can convince anybody in the world.'

His new career allows him to put a fresh spin on his old tricks: handing out gym vouchers to women, having sex with students in the dressing room. His work does not pay much, so he is always on the lookout for a quick buck or a free meal. 'It gets tiring,' says Dror Niv. 'If you come in my restaurant and I let you eat for free, you can't – you shouldn't – take liberties. But people still like him. Old times, you know?'

Kaiser has found other ways to earn money. He befriended a plastic surgeon and became a middleman for breast-enhancement jobs, taking commission on every customer he recommended. He also had two fiancées in the same gym, with one working out in the morning and the other in the afternoon. When one of them found underwear from a third woman on Kaiser's couch, the whole thing unravelled.

Kaiser's other students knew about his double engagement and played along. 'It was very tricky,' says Manuela, one of Kaiser's students. 'It was really funny, too. Bonkers. He's an emperor!'

\*\*\*

One framed photograph sits alone on a wall in Kaiser's apartment. It was taken in Búzios in the mid-1990s, and shows Kaiser crouching alongside his second son and Renato Gaúcho. 'That really touches me,' says Renato. 'It makes me really happy and from that you can see his character. You can see that I've been friends with him ever since I met him. It wasn't fleeting. So it's a recognition of the family that he didn't have. That flatters me. That makes me happy and very moved.'

The wallpaper on his phone is the picture with Renato Gaúcho and Gaúcho at the Brahma beer launch. He has bags full of reminders of his youth – all the newspaper articles, photos and videos. There is also an article about Marcella, taken from a glossy magazine. It has the stamp of Pergus, the gym from which it was stolen.

Nostalgia is Kaiser's best friend and his worst enemy. He is in a tortured limbo, a twentysomething trapped in a fiftysomething's body. He struggles to accept that the party is over; that he will never again be the King of Rio. Kaiser has become accustomed to death. But he will never stop grieving the loss of his youth.

# CHAPTER 33

# THE ENIGMA

Kaiser wants to make one thing clear. 'I did this book,' he says, 'to tell the truth.' But in Brazil there are many truths, many truths. Kaiser's memory is somewhere between selective and defective and there is an undeniable element of fantasy to his tale. His story requires not only the suspension of disbelief but also of modern attitudes – Rio in the eighties and nineties was a very different place to the Western world in 2018.

The more you look into his story, the more one thing becomes clear: a lot of this stuff really did happen.

'If you tell somebody from abroad about Kaiser, they will call you a liar,' says Gil, the former Brazil forward and Botafogo manager. 'But everyone involved in football in

Rio de Janeiro knows about him. He's a professional con man. He found a way to make a living through lying. I think he's the only person on the planet who for twenty-six years played football without putting on a pair of boots. He doesn't even know that the ball is round.'

Everybody has a different take on what did or did not happen. 'I'm not sure about some of his stories,' says the dentist Ricardo Ostenhas. 'I could have a Real Madrid ID card here from when I was twenty years old. Where's the proof? Are there photos or footage? But I saw him training at Fluminense; I saw him walk off with the beautiful girl that everybody wanted. Ah, Kaiser, you're a real character, man. Fuck me.'

One person will tell you he was at Independiente at Argentina, another that he has never had a passport and simply took advantage of the fact they already had a player called Carlos Enrique. 'I believe he was at Independiente,' says Marcio Meira, the Fluminense fitness coach. 'I believe he found some way to be there because he is phenomenal. In that respect he *is* Maradona. If he told me that he was hanging out with the Argentinian squad at the World Cup I'd believe it. I just don't believe he played.'

There are a number of credible sources who place Kaiser at Vasco, Botafogo, Fluminense, Bangu, America, Cruzeiro, Flamengo and Palmeiras at various points in the 1980s and 1990s. His official Brazilian Football Confederation player book has contracts for the last two, while he also has official prescriptions for anti-inflammatories from Fluminense and Vasco.

In an attempt to stress the scale of Kaiser's deception, his old friend Adriano Dias Oliveira breaks excitedly into pidgin English. 'Arsenal! Tottenham! Chelsea! He sign! Sign contracts! Never play!'

Bangu openly admit that Kaiser was with the club in two spells, in the mid-1980s and again in 1994. Some other clubs are not so forthcoming. A few have issued po-faced denials of Kaiser's presence, even if their story is contradicted by ex-players or employees. 'It's something that doesn't sound that good,' says Júnior Negão. 'A professional football team having a player who never played. So as the years have passed, the owners end up denying everything, saying it was a hoax or a rumour. They don't want to be associated with his story.'

Kaiser paints himself as a variation on Robin Hood, getting something back for the players who had been treated badly by chairmen. 'It doesn't surprise me that they deny I was there. There has always been a core of directors for whom I didn't pay dividends on the field. Some got over that; some didn't. A lot of them talk as if it were a son who's let down his father. They prefer to forget that Kaiser existed. Every club I've been at probably won't admit it because I was a disappointment for them. But clubs screw so many people over that somebody had to trick the clubs. I was a trailblazer – a superhero for the players, because I didn't screw them over. While chairmen were exploiting players in Brazil and all over the world, I was exploiting them. You can't buy a torch and say that it doesn't turn on because you won't be able to sell it on. All the teams I went to celebrated twice. Once when I signed and then again when I left. The only exception to that was Bangu.'

Fabinho, the former Ajaccio forward, saw Kaiser go through the departure lounge for a flight to Texas to play for El Paso; Fabinho's brother saw him sign for Bangu. 'Listen,' says Fabinho. 'There are some true things. I saw him train at Fluminense – just training, I never saw him play. I don't know if he had a contract there. He trained at Vasco, too. He did actually go to El Paso. I think he was at Palmeiras. I heard from many people that was pretty much how the Bangu story went. But Independiente in Argentina is another total fabrication just like Ajaccio. I don't believe anything about Puebla either.'

Alexandre Torres, Renato Gaúcho and Ricardo Rocha have a simple rule to determine whether Kaiser is telling the truth. If the story is on the field, it's a lie; if it's off the field, it's true. 'I believe everything,' says Ricardo Rocha. 'That he had an orgy with the prime minister. I believe he went to big clubs like he says. There's only one thing I don't believe: that he played football. I'm not quite sure about that. I'm aware of his problems with the ball. He has a serious problem. He's very good at everything else. Send him a kiss and a hug. A great friend.'

It's tempting to assume some of the more extreme stories, like his fight with the fans at Bangu, were fabricated. But Marcelo Henrique, a ballboy that day, remembers it all in detail.

Many of Kaiser's friends don't even know his real name is Carlos. His nickname has accompanied him ever since he was compared to Franz Beckenbauer. Luiz Maerovitch says he was given the name because he was chubby and resembled a beer bottle. The real truth could be any variation of both stories. Kaiser beer did not exist until 1980, so it's possible Maerovitch and his friends took an established nickname and gave it a different origin; or it might be that Kaiser was given that nickname in the 1980s and created his own backstory.

Most aspects of Kaiser's life have a similar ambiguity that is as fascinating as it is frustrating. Just when you think you have a handle on the truth, something contradicts it. Kaiser was useless at football? Jair Pereira, manager of Atlético Madrid, says he was talented. Kaiser never went abroad? Fabinho, who blew holes in the Ajaccio story, saw him board a flight to El Paso.

It's natural to assume Kaiser did not have the talent to be spotted by Botafogo as a child, but he has a dog-eared old ID card that looks like it came straight out of 1977, and includes a picture of a child who strongly resembles the adult Kaiser. It looks impossible to fake, but with Kaiser you never quite know.

There are also photos of Kaiser with stars of Brazilian football like Carlos Alberto Torres, Edmundo and Maurício – not to mention hundreds with Renato Gaúcho. They are natural and authentic, not staged like the ones with the Brazilian World Cup squad of 1986.

Some are more sceptical than others about Kaiser's stories. Dror Niv, the restaurateur, takes everything with a massive pinch of salt. 'When I met him in 1986 he was in good shape,' he says. 'He once told me that he went on a diet and lost forty kilos. So when did he lose these forty kilos? I asked some people who knew him as a teenager and they said he was fat then. So if he lost forty kilos, which youth team did he play for? If he's seventy-five kilos now he must have been a hundred and fifteen kilos as a teenager. Explain the maths for me. It doesn't fly.'

*\*\**

Most of Kaiser's friends don't believe his suggestion that sex was his only motivation for being a footballer. They think he was desperate to be a professional but was born without the necessary talent, and settled for the next best thing. The access to women was a happy consequence of that and served to fuel his ego. 'He wasn't addicted to sex like a famous actor,' says Alexandre Couto. 'His obsession with sex was all about his own image, and how people would see him. He wanted to show off that he was capable of pulling the most attractive women.'

How often he did so is also open to debate. 'He says he's slept with over a thousand women,' smiles Ricardo Rocha. 'That's a fantasy of his, to be like Renato. He's got the gift of the gab. If it doesn't work, that's fine. He's like a fisherman: he throws his net out, waits for a couple of hours and if a little fish swims in, he reels it in. But a thousand fish? I'm not having that.'

There are others who think 1,000 is a conservative estimate. The truth is out there somewhere, but nobody knows where to find it.

\*\*\*

The most gut-wrenching part of Kaiser's story, the death of Marcella Mendes, is confirmed by everyone – even Dror Niv, who questions everything that comes out of Kaiser's mouth. 'I'm not certain she was his wife,' he says, 'but they were definitely together and she did die.'

He is less convinced about the fate of Kaiser's son. 'I don't think his son existed,' he says. 'That's why he had to die.' Others think Kaiser has no contact with him, and so his son – like the other two fiancées Kaiser mentioned – is dead in a metaphorical sense. 'You can never tell if it's true or not,' says Alexandre Couto. 'We never know whether to laugh or cry!'

Alexandre also has a theory about Kaiser's backstory; that he says he was stolen in Porto Alegre so that he could claim he was a Gaúcho who became a Carioca – just like Renato Gaúcho.

\*\*\*

And then there's Ajaccio. Kaiser will acknowledge all his football-related lies, but on this he does not give an inch. He says Fabinho is lying and Alexandre Couto tells the truth. And Alexandre Couto did support Kaiser's version – but only the first time he was interviewed.

'He thinks he was there, that he played and everything,' says Fabinho. 'But there's no concrete proof. It would be good to ask him, "Show me a photo of you and somebody else on the Ajaccio pitch", or "Show me a photo of you training with the Ajaccio players". There isn't one. If you call the club and ask if there was a Brazilian called Fabio Barros from 1986 to 1991 they will confirm that I was there. I'm solid proof. Alexandre Couto was there, too. He was actually referred by me.'

Many of Kaiser's friends think he has played a game of Chinese whispers for so long that he has somehow brainwashed himself to the point where he no longer knows what is true and what is not. 'A lot of things he would actually believe as if they happened,' says Gustavo. 'You could put him under bright lights and interrogate him and he would go the distance. And he won't stray from what he says. If you can get away with it, why not? And he got away with it!'

If Kaiser doesn't know what did or did not happen, everybody else has no chance.

*\*\**

Two of the things that make Kaiser's story so slippery are his propensity to answer a different question from the one that has been asked, and the absence of a firm timeline. 'Living in the past is for history teachers,' he says. On one occasion, after being nagged once too often, he barked, 'I'm not a talking calendar!' Yet he can recite the telephone number of a Búzios hotel he stayed in twenty years ago.

'Don't ask me, "What about this game?"' says Kaiser. 'For fuck's sake. I stopped playing in 2003, and I'm going to speak about a certain game? That's tricky. "Oh, that goal you scored." Come on. Romário scored a thousand goals. I don't care if I scored one goal.'

It's unlikely he ever got on the field in an official match, even if it is sometimes reported that he played around thirty professional games. All the reports agree on one detail: that he scored no goals. 'If he had gone on the field he wouldn't have as much prestige as he does now,' says Ricardo Ostenhas. 'He would just be another rubbish player.'

Rio has never been the most anal of places: people live in the moment rather than treating life like a judicial review. 'I honestly don't care about the context of Kaiser's story and what is true or not,' says Marco Tioco, who helped bring it to light in 2011. 'I thought that Bangu story was a lie, but other players have confirmed that it happened. It doesn't really matter to me. It doesn't change the context of his story.'

Some things have no explanation at all. The famous Ajaccio photoshoot, taken at Clube dos Macacos, includes some pictures of Kaiser in the shirt of the Austrian club Wacker Innsbruck. Fabinho and Alexandre Couto are sure they did not give that shirt to Kaiser, while Kaiser's version – that he swapped it during a pre-season friendly with Ajaccio – can probably go in the dustbin.

'I think the charming thing about it is that we don't actually know what happened,' says Júnior Negão. 'It's that ambiguity, which he sustained for many years. That's his whole charm. Kaiser has a lot of stories, and those stories create the legend. You end up enjoying them because after telling the same lie four times it basically becomes the truth. So all his stories might as well be true. His story has now been eternalised.'

The story has a few more chapters left. For a 171, the hustle never ends. 'In the context of the character he created, he's a genius,' says Renato Mendes Mota. 'If Kaiser didn't have that character I don't think he'd even be alive today. He needed that in order to survive in Rio de Janeiro.'

\*\*\*

The Wikipedia page for the 1984 Intercontinental Cup final between Independiente and Liverpool was changed in December 2017. There was an amendment to the list of Independiente substitutes, with the addition of somebody called Carlos Henrique Raposo. The edit history showed the IP address through which the change had been made. The location of that IP address?

Rio de Janeiro.

In April 2018, a cinematic documentary about Kaiser premiered at Tribeca Film Festival in New York. The festival was co-founded by Robert De Niro, so maybe Kaiser did get to go to the after-party with him.

The film included dramatisations, in which an actor called Eduardo Lara played the role of Kaiser. His performance was not entirely to Kaiser's taste. 'You have to teach the actor how a football player goes down on their knees when they're playing,' he says. 'You can tell by the way they walk whether they're a player or not. He might play badminton but he doesn't play football. A real footballer will always know if somebody is pretending to be a footballer.'

It's a delicious twist that the internet and a greater circulation of knowledge, the things that would have stopped Kaiser's con at a stroke in the eighties and early nineties, have now given him a second wind. There have been articles about him in more than twenty countries, including prestigious publications like *France Football*, *Der Spiegel* in Germany and the *Guardian* in England. Each interview means a bit more money for Kaiser, and the chance to tell stories about the stories. It's the grift that keeps on giving.

The extent of Kaiser's deception is mind-blowing. A lot of his scams were fairly normal in Rio, but only Kaiser had the nerve and verve to pull them off on an industrial scale. 'It's impossible to conceive how he did all that,' says the singer Bebeto. 'The guy is either a genius or incredibly brave. I think he's a genius. You need to open his brain up and study it, like they did with Einstein.'

Kaiser is a cross between Pelé, Frank Abagnale and Walter Mitty. He did not build a football career through lying; he built a whole life. His existence is a mosaic of small fibs that have made up one huge lie. That is the legend of Carlos Kaiser: the man whose life is based on a true story.

# ACKNOWLEDGEMENTS

There are loads of people I need to thank for their help with this book, so here goes: Gregg Bakowski, Alex Bellos, Will Billany, James Dart, Cris Freddi, Olivia Gannon, Tim Goddard, Daniel Harris, Laura McManamon, Steve Middleditch, Ray Mills, Alex Netherton, Alex Perkins, Richard Pike, James Pollard, Ian Smyth, Stewart Till, Steve Williams and Ed Wilson. Most of all, I'd like to thank and apologise to those I've inevitably forgotten to include in this list.

Rob Bagchi, Paul Doyle, Mike Gibbons, Daniel Harris and Scott Murray were full of sound advice, while every chat with Tim de Lisle made me want to attack a blank page.

I'll always be grateful to Don McRae for introducing me to the weird world of Kaiser, and to Tom Markham, Rob Fullam, Stefan Choynowski and Louis Myles for asking me to write the book. Their support and ideas, especially when I was going mad trying to work out a timeline of Kaiser's life, were invaluable.

In Brazil, Eduardo Pagnoncelli, Roberta Fortuna, Daniele Mazzer, Mariana Pinto, Martha Esteves, Paula Lima, Fernanda Rizzo and Reinaldo Borges Campos were indispensable and did everything from translating to driving. Without them, this would be a pamphlet rather than a book.

All the interviewees were generous both with their time and their memories of Kaiser. Every audience with Kaiser was memorable for all kinds of reasons.

It's been a pleasure to work with everyone at Yellow Jersey – thanks to Richard Collins, Rowena Skelton-Wallace, Sally Sargeant, Joe Pickering, Sophie Painter, Matt Broughton, who designed such a brilliant cover, and especially Tim Broughton.

Most of all, thanks to Jay, Royal, Eli and Ethel for their love, support and silliness.